THE CIVIL WAR DIARY OF CYRUS F. BOYD

FIFTEENTH IOWA INFANTRY

1861-1863

Edited by
MILDRED THRONE

New Introduction by
E.B. LONG

KRAUS REPRINT CO.

Millwood, N.Y.

1977

This work was originally published in the
Iowa Journal of History. Volume 50, 1952.

973.781

B69c

101148

may 1977

Library of Congress Cataloging in Publication Data

Boyd, Cyrus F.
  The Civil War Diary of Cyrus F. Boyd, Fifteenth Iowa
Infantry 1861-1863.

  Reprint of the ed. published by the State Historical
Society of Iowa, Iowa City.
  1. United States—History—Civil War, 1861-1865—
Regimental histories—Iowa Infantry—15th. 2. Iowa
Infantry. 15th Regiment, 1862-1865. 3. United States—
History—Civil War, 1861-1865—Personal narratives.
4. Boyd, Cyrus F. I. Title.
E507.5 15th.B68   1976   973.7'81   76-44635
ISBN 0-527-17540-4

Reprinted with permission of
The State Historical Society of Iowa
KRAUS REPRINT CO.
A U.S. Division of Kraus-Thomson Organization Limited

Printed in U.S.A.

NEW INTRODUCTION

It was the greatest adventure possible for a young American of the 1860s. It was an opportunity to see and experience much beyond the narrow confines of his village, county, or ingrown urban area. It was a chance to grow up, to enlarge horizons, to travel, to share in momentous events. And, although he may not have realized it, it was an open door to an education he could never have received within his own limited purview.

This is how Cyrus F. Boyd of the 15th Iowa Volunteer Infantry saw the American Civil War, as disclosed in the words of his diary. It was how thousands of other soldiers, from both North and South, wrote of their individual microcosm of war in their diaries and letters during the conflict. And this is how those who made it back home wrote about it in the years that followed.

Union or Confederate army service was a never-never world— new, unique, exhilarating, exciting. Some understood why they were fighting, or thought they did. Others did not know, but went along, for it was the patriotic thing to do and there were strong pressures to enlist. But if they thought they knew why they were fighting, few knew when they signed up what they were to do, how to do it, or what they were to face. And perhaps this was just as well. Yet the vast majority were determined to make the most of this new life, this mission, this crusade.

About 3,000,000 Yankees and Southerners were engaged in the war. Some 600,000 of them were killed in battle, were mortally wounded or died of disease. The war was big, by far the biggest, most traumatic, and all-encompassing event in the history of the country. Between 1861 and 1865 there were roughly 1,500 days of war. There were 10,455 military events of one size or another, from mighty battles in which tens of thousands were involved to small-scale skirmishes. Most of the nation was involved, but the

NEW INTRODUCTION

main areas were the Eastern Seaboard, the Mississippi Valley, and all of the South.

The soldier diaries and letters left to us naturally vary greatly in quality and in extensiveness of description, yet there is a telling similarity of expression. It is this similarity, though each writer conveys his individuality, that gives us the feeling that we are getting a comparatively accurate view of what it was like to go asoldiering in the 1860s.

Cyrus F. Boyd's is one of those narratives we can feel safe in relying on for an account of what life was like in the army and for a fascinating slice of social history. He reveals much that other soldiers reveal but often does it more effectively. Observant, sensitively aware of the dramatic happenings around him, yet balanced, Boyd seems to have been in little danger of exaggerating.

Caught up in the dynamic force of events, Boyd naively marched off to war along with many young men from his small corner of Iowa near Indianola, south of Des Moines. The shock of entering the world beyond south central Iowa was mitigated a bit, as it was for most Civil War soldiers, by the fact that a large portion of his regiment came from the same area. Thus the men had the advantage of being in effect part of a traveling extension of their home community, the regiment becoming in a small way a home away from home.

Yet this camaraderie had its disadvantages. Voting for regimental officers, particularly in the early days of the war, often resembled a rowdy hometown election characterized by jealousy, rough competition, gossip, and intrigue.

Company G of the 15th Iowa was mustered in at Keokuk on the Mississippi River during the late fall and early winter of 1861. In March of 1862 it was sent to Benton Barracks south of St. Louis for what passed for more training.

Cyrus Boyd is detailed and forthright in recounting this early period of his war adventures. The reader relives with him the trials and pleasures of camp life. No one soldier could see more than a minute segment of this gigantic tapestry of war. But if he managed to survive the bullets, even if only at one or two battles, he had plenty to write home about. With wisdom and insight, Boyd wrote that a soldier's province is "quite limited in War, confined to the narrow bounds of a few companions and the little orbit in which he moves." He compares his life to "a spoke in a great wheel moved by the motion of some great invisible power."

He is lyrical also in expressions of patriotism, emphasizing the purity of his motives and his proud sense of duty. This genuine

NEW INTRODUCTION

outpouring of patriotic emotion seems to have motivated the majority of soldiers, at least at first. Boyd writes boyishly from Keokuk, "We may be going to see all we want to before the row is over but here goes for glory or for fun."

The winter in Keokuk seemed a lively one for the young soldier. As an orderly sergeant (who won his post by the flip of a coin) he had a somewhat remarkable social life, being entertained in many homes, particularly those where the families included young ladies. However, Boyd worried about the morals of his fellow soldiers. At Benton Barracks he complained, "There seems to be no Sunday here. There seems to be no God here but more than an average amount of the Devil."

On April 1, 1862, the regiment pulled away by steamer from Benton Barracks, the band playing "Dixie," to "enter the dark land of secession and the enemies home." And it was a dark world indeed, soon to be broken by the manmade lightning flash of war. On Sunday, April 6, amid the blossoming peach trees along the Tennessee River, the battle-green 15th Iowa, having only received their arms, heard the early-morning opening guns of what was to be known to history as the Battle of Shiloh or Pittsburg Landing.

The exact role of Boyd, Company G, or the 15th Iowa during two April days, just where they stood or where they moved, doesn't really matter. What does matter is that here in an unknown land a group of scared Iowa farm boys, led by neophyte officers, faced a cataclysm of fire, fury, and death such as none of these civilian soldiers could have imagined. Here in southern Tennessee every man, in blue or in gray, grew up in a hurry. Here luck, in its ugliest and most enigmatic form, played its macabre role.

One can walk today through the woods and fields and along the roads of Shiloh. At first it may seem a quiet and tranquil place. But soon a crescendo mounts, the eyes are dimmed, and we perceive echoes, faint though they may be, of at least a little of what Sergeant Boyd lived through in those distant days. "No pen can tell, no hand can paint, no words can utter the horrors of last night," Boyd wrote on the second day of battle "on this field of *death*."

These pages are not pleasant reading; they cannot be. We share Boyd's sense of revulsion and his morbid fascination with the anguish and carnage he lived through. Even to one who has read scores, if not hundreds, of Civil War battle accounts, this poignant recital cannot help but bring an intense sense of sorrow and a chilling to the soul.

The youthful sergeant, overwhelmed with emotion, tells us, "War is *hell* broke *loose* and benumbs all the tender feelings of men and makes them *brutes*. I do not want to see any more such scenes and yet I would not have missed this for any consideration." The adventure, the growing up, the education, the insight into the human heart. He would not have missed this hell!

Boyd's diary contains moving and accurate descriptions of himself and his regiment through the summer march on Corinth, Mississippi, and into the fall of 1862. He describes what he saw of the unsuccessful Confederate effort to retake Corinth. Through the winter of 1862-1863, and the early abortive attempts against Vicksburg, the Confederate bastion on the Mississippi, he perceptively relates the personal story of one average soldier.

Boyd concludes his narrative in March of 1863 when he finally obtains a commission as second lieutenant in the 34th Iowa Infantry. He is pleased with his commission, but as he departs for a new "home" he thinks of the companions in arms he will have to leave and regrets that he "could not but realize that I should rather be a non-commissioned officer with such *friends* than to be at the head of any Regiment *without* them."

As did many soldiers, Boyd wrote candidly. He grew to dislike his regimental commander, Colonel Hugh T. Reid. He could also write that "General Grant is hated and *despised* by all the men and cursed ever since the 6th of April."

As was prevalent with soldiers, he could on occasion do a bit of foraging for supplies; he was often sick but had to march anyway; he learned, as did so many, the curative powers of blackberries; he was disgusted with interregimental politics that temporarily denied him rank. He was alternately buoyed up and depressed by Union victories and defeats elsewhere; he was appalled at the practices of the sutlers, merchants who followed the army "like buzzards"; he described the numerous blacks who flocked to the Union lines; and he wrote on November 15, 1862, in disillusionment, "This war is getting to be a stupendous humbug." He expressed concern over the whisky drinking of the men; he stoically endured tiresome marches that often went nowhere and appeared to mean nothing. He tells of rumors, of the increasing attrition in the company, all of which are part of almost every soldier's story.

With the everlasting and innate curiosity of the American soldier, he toured battlefields just hours after the firing had stopped. There is throughout Boyd's account a disarming quality of authenticity and discernment, of immediacy that only one who had "been there"—or, in the soldier parlance of the time, one who had "seen the elephant"—can give.

By 1863 he expressed a feeling of hopelessness. "Discouragements are thick and heavy upon all this army . . . We are having a

NEW INTRODUCTION

poor Policy of carrying on the War or a poor way of executing a good Policy. . . . " Boyd shows he is near to graduating from the school of war: "The hog pens in Iowa do not get in a worse condition than our camp ground. One year ago such times as these would have made us all sick. But we are pretty tough and are not much affected by such small matters. When we landed at Pittsburgh [sic] we knew nothing about soldiering. We could not cook and we could not eat. . . . The experiences of these days learned us much. . . . "

In a fuller context Boyd comments that "the times look gloomy and the darkness that surrounds the Republic can almost be felt." By the beginning of 1863 Boyd is more conscious than ever of "this hellish system of human slavery. . . . "

The late Dr. Mildred Throne of the State Historical Society of Iowa performed an admirable job as editor of Boyd's diary. Never intruding, she deftly supplied the few needed details to amplify the story. Dr. Throne contributed much to studies of the Civil War through her sympathetic and expert work on Boyd's and numerous other diaries. The State Historical Society of Iowa was fortunate to obtain this diary and must be congratulated for first bringing it to print. Boyd's spelling and punctuation have been retained.

What makes Boyd's account of a year and a half of war in a portion of the west of the Mississippi Valley important is not that his story is different from many others. Indeed, it is quite typical. Its special importance today is that he writes his experiences openly, simply, and intimately. Probably never intended for publication and meant only for the eyes of friends, Boyd's trenchant chronicle has as much meaning and significance for us today as it had to the soldiers of the Civil War. His emotions, his prejudices, his disgust and wonderment are here. We feel we know him; for a few hours, at least, we can march, rest, and fight with him and his companions of the 1860s. We are transported out of our everyday life, as were Boyd and his fellow soldiers in 1861, to enter momentarily a terrible and fascinating world, a world that usually seems unreal and distant. The sights and sounds, the amazement, the abhorrence, the anguish, and the "fun" are evoked for us to share. And Cyrus F. Boyd has told us the truth about his wartime days. For he was there.

E.B.LONG

Laramie, Wyoming

CONTENTS

ILLUSTRATIONS

INTRODUCTION

In 1951 the State Historical Society of Iowa came into possession of an unusually fine Civil War diary — that of Cyrus F. Boyd of Company G, Fifteenth Iowa Volunteer Infantry. This is not the ordinary camp and battlefield diary, with brief entries of only the highlights of the day. Boyd kept such a diary, but after the war, in the peace and quiet of home, he took these "several small memorandum" and from them compiled his "Daily Journal."

One of Boyd's closest friends was Daniel Embree of Indianola, Iowa. In 1896, when a resident of Ainsworth, Nebraska, Boyd sent a copy of his diary to his friend Dan with the note: "The enclosed copy from my Journal may be of interest to you as the years go by." The diary remained in the possession of the Embree family until 1951, when Daniel's daughter, Bertha Embree Dodds, died in California. It then came into the hands of Mrs. Dodds's attorney, Kuno Doerr of South Pasadena. At the suggestion of his nephew, Edward Doerr of Davenport, Mr. Doerr presented the diary to the State Historical Society for preservation. It was originally published serially in the Society's quarterly, *Iowa Journal of History*, in the four issues of 1952 (Volume 50).

Cyrus F. Boyd was twenty-four years old at the time of his enlistment in Company G of the Fifteenth Iowa Infantry; his friend, Dan, was twenty-one. Boyd served as Orderly Sergeant in Company G until March 14, 1863, when he resigned to accept a commission as First Lieutenant in Company B of the Thirty-fourth Iowa Infantry. He was mustered out of service on November 12, 1864. Embree served throughout his term of enlistment in Company G of the Fifteenth, being mustered in as Sixth Corporal. After successive promotions he was commissioned Second Lieutenant on March 7,

1863, First Lieutenant on August 27, 1864, and was mustered out on December 20, 1864.

The diary is an extremely full account of soldiering in the Union Army, written from the point of view of an outspoken "citizen soldier," who did not hesitate to express his opinions of his comrades and his officers, who described with frankness and many touches of humor the conditions of camp life and camp living, and who in simple, often startling, language wrote descriptions of battles and their terrible aftermath that call to mind comparisons with modern realistic writing. Much of the diary is not pleasant reading, but it is an honest, simple account of one man's experiences in a bloody civil conflict, and as such is worthy of preservation.

MILDRED THRONE

Associate Editor,
State Historical Society of Iowa,
Iowa City, Iowa.

PART I

INDIANOLA, IOWA, TO PITTSBURG LANDING, TENNESSEE

October 15, 1861 to April 7, 1862

The Battle of Shiloh

CYRUS F. BOYD'S DAILY JOURNAL [1]

This book is compiled from the notes of several small memorandum carried in the pocket and which were kept from the date of my enlistment in the Army that was raised to put down the Great Rebellion of 1861.

The design being to keep a record of what was seen and experienced by myself during the trials of those bloody years which followed Very little in this Journal will be known to History as it shall be written here — as one's own province is quite limited in War, confined to the narrow bounds of a few companions and the little orbit in which he moves, Like a spoke in a great wheel moved by the motion of some great invisible power and not permitted to know why or wherefore he is expected to perform his part in the great work.

This will also aim to record the doings and the fate of many of my companions Having escaped the uncertain fates of War and lived to record my own part in the great struggle is sufficient satisfaction to warrant me in spending the time in consolidating the notes and memoranda which throughout the term of three years and four months was a *daily* duty I scarcely ever omitted even in the most unfavorable circumstances of making a note of all of interest that occured [sic] around me along our tedoius and perilous pathway

[1] For the service records of Cyrus F. Boyd and his friend, Daniel Embree, see *Roster and Record of Iowa Soldiers in the War of the Rebellion* . . . (6 vols., Des Moines, 1908–1911), 2:911, 936; 5:271. (Hereafter listed as *Roster Iowa Soldiers*.)

A note book in my side pocket was like a pocket knife always at command on the march and a larger book in camp or in the baggage was written up at the first opportunity

During the Presidential campaign of 1860 several of us boys around
Palmyra in Warren County Iowa, organized a company of young men just
young and strong enough to do some tall yelling. We were mounted on
horses. Our uniforms consisted of a pair of blue overalls — a white waist
and a chip hat. The total cost of a uniform was about 85 cents. We each
had a horse or rather a *colt*. We not only had to break and drill ourselves
but had to break the *colts* also and at the same time. We were supposed to
be assisting Abraham Lincoln to be elected President and everybody now
knows that he was elected We did not do him harm enough to prevent his
election over Breckenridge and Douglas

Our Company was composed of about thirty boys all on farms in the
immediate neighborhood At the organization of the Company I was elected
Captain We carried a banner and on it was inscribed the following

"Lincoln   Hamlin"
and
"Victory"

Above the banner and inserted in the flag staff were several little mauls
and wedges We attended all the Rallies in that County and some outside
and when our man Lincoln called for men to suppress the insurrection we
did not respond the first time but at the next call we left the colts at home
and went almost to [a] *boy*.[2]

Indianola Iowa

Oct 15th, 1861. To-day I took my little squad of boys who are left of
the Lincoln campaign to Indianola We have made up our minds to enlist
for the War Times are dull at home and many have gone at the call of the
President and joined the different Regiments from the State

A long and lonesome Winter is coming on and the War may be over by
spring and we should feel as if we had lost a great deal by not going and if

[2] Lincoln's first call for troops was on April 15, 1861; Iowa was requested to furnish one regiment, to serve for 100 days. Further calls for troops, for three-year en-
listments, came on May 3 (answered by the 2nd through the 7th Iowa regiments),
July 23 (8th through 13th Iowa regiments), and in October (14th through 17th Iowa
regiments). Thus, it would appear that Boyd and his "boys" did not answer the
second, but rather the *fourth* call of the President. Jacob A. Swisher, *Iowa in Times
of War* (Iowa City, 1943), 77, 80-81.

the war should last longer we will have the credit of not waiting until we were pushed out Every one seems to be actuated by the purest and most patriotic motives and those who are going seem to be moved by a sense of duty.

I had a long talk with Dr Fisk.[3] He talks very strongly of enlisting, and thinks he can raise a Company if I will turn my squad in with him Lewis Todhunter saw me with Fisk and called me into his office and warned me to be careful about forming any alliance with Fisk. Said he that man Fisk was raised a "democrat" and he may betray you somewhere when you are in a tight place But few men have any confidence in him said Mr Todhunter and you had better keep your men well in hand as I am going to raise a company of *artillery* "they use cannon" and you can join my company and be 1st Lieutenant Right here my patience with Mr Todhunter oozed out and I plainly told him that of the two men I should choose Dr Fisk in pref- erence — I told him I did not believe he intended to enlist and that I be- lieved his only object was to discourage us from going so that he would have more company at home[4]

Fisk thinks if we cannot raise a Company here we can join some other squad to make out the number and has heard of a part of a company at Knoxville that is unable to complete its number of men He will go to Knoxville tonight on the stage to see about it

Oct 17th Fisk has returned and reports about 50 men at Knoxville who are anxious to have us join them We will go to-morrow in wagons

Knoxville Jowa

Oct 18th Bid the folks *good-bye* at Palmyra last eve and came to Indian- ola To-day we started in wagons for Knoxville some twenty of us Had a long hard days drive and arrived at the Judkins House late and got our sup- pers Bundy of Indianola came with us He is an intimate friend of Dr Fisk and is a jolly fat man to be with Have oysters after supper and Bundy

[3] Hezekiah Fisk was thirty-six years old in 1861; he was elected First Lieutenant of Company G, 15th Iowa; received various promotions; was captured at Shiloh; appointed Assistant Surgeon, March 7, 1863; died August 19, 1864, of wounds re- ceived at Atlanta. *Roster Jowa Soldiers*, 2:942.

[4] Cyrus Boyd was a man of very strong likes and dislikes, as will be shown in this diary. Lewis Todhunter was a prominent attorney of Indianola and had served in the constitutional convention of 1857 which re-wrote Iowa's constitution. During the Civil War he was an Assistant Quartermaster with the rank of Captain. Following Lee's surrender, he served as Post Quartermaster at Richmond, Virginia, until Sep- tember, 1865. *History of Warren County, Jowa* . . . (Des Moines, 1879), 605-606.

stands the treat I was born too far from the sea shore so I do not take oysters Retired at 12 M

Oct *19th* Got acquainted with several Knoxville men this morning Was introduced to a man named Wm T Cunningham[5] who they say will be Captain of the new Company I like his appearance very much He is a fine looking man and all speak well of him He is full of anecdotes and jokes and of very easy manners Is about 5 feet 10 in in height — sandy complexion and weighs about 175 lbs.

Was introduced to a man by the name of Hanks[6] who was in the Mexican War and who will probably be 1st Lieut. He is a thin wiry man with a prominent nose and of a very *confidential* turn He flattered me quite lively by saying that he had made a good deal of enquiry about me among the Indianola boys and also among their own men who had seen me and they all seemed anxious that I should be one of the commissioned officers of the new company He further said that Fisk wanted the place but that the Knoxville boys "did not like his ways" My reply was that I cared nothing about the Commission Was not going for honor or pay but would be willing to give way to any good man

A man by the name of Ethridge is talked of for one of the officers Met at the Court House after dinner — A large crowd was there with drums and music The crowd filed into the Court House and the meeting was called to order Proceeded to ballot for officers Wm T Cunningham was elected Captain without opposition R. L. Hanks and Dr Fisk were candidates for 1st Lieut Hanks was elected Fisk was elected 2d Lieut and all our squad were glad Now came the election of 1st or Orderly Sergeant David Myers[7] of Knoxville was mentioned and my name also It looked as if there would be a division about equal between the two sections of the two counties Myers having been a candidate for 2d Lieut and defeated came to me and proposed that we *cast lots* as to which of us should be the

[5] William T. Cunningham, born in Virginia, was thirty-six when appointed Captain, Company G, 15th Iowa. He was promoted to Major, Aug. 1, 1862; wounded at Corinth, Oct. 3, 1862; resigned at Memphis, Jan. 16, 1863. *Roster Iowa Soldiers*, 2:923.

[6] Romulus L. Hanks of Knoxville, a native of Kentucky, was thirty-nine years old at the time of his enlistment as First Lieutenant. He was promoted Captain Aug. 1, 1862, wounded slightly at Corinth on Oct. 3, 1862, and resigned Aug. 26, 1864. *Ibid.*, 2:958.

[7] David Myers, of Knoxville, native of Kentucky, age twenty-eight, transferred to Co. K, 15th Iowa, Feb. 18, 1862. *Ibid.*, 2:991.

Candidate while the other withdrew Having consented Myers proposed to throw up a *silver half dollar* He gave me choice and I said "tails" — as tails it would probably be *Tails* came up and here commenced my military troubles Was unanimously elected The captain congratulated me and also many of the men I think we have a good company

Oct 20th This is Sunday. Am staying at a Mr French's house with two or three of the boys All the people seem very kind and every house is open to us Attended church at the Presbyterian

Oct 21st Started in wagons for Eddyville this morning The day was wet and cold and the roads quite muddy The people of Knoxville cheered us and waved flags rags and handkerchiefs to us as we went out of town

Oct 22d We stoped at the Amos House in Eddyville last night or rather this morning having got lodging at Bellefountaine[8] some miles back on the Des Moines river The proprietor of the Amos is said to be a violent old "copper head" I am sure he must hate a Union soldier from quality of the fare he set out to us this morning.

Keokuk Iowa

Oct 23d This evening we arrived at Keokuk via the Des Moines Valley Railroad.[9] It was dark when we arrived at the Depot. We were taken off the cars like a drove of swine: the men yelling and cheering at the top of their voices We took up a random line of march through the City on and on until we are upon a high bluff outside the limits of the town and among some old board shanties or Barracks where we are told that we can lodge for the night Who brought us here I can not tell The wind howls fearfully and the air is frosty and bitter cold. We call this a little tough to commence

---

[8] Bellefontaine, in Scott Township, Mahaska County, was laid out in 1846; when the railroad built through the county in the 1870's it built a station at Tracy, in Marion County, about three-quarters of a mile away, thus ending the existence of Bellefontaine. *History of Mahaska County, Iowa* . . . (Des Moines, 1878), 533; John W. Wright and W. A. Young (eds.), *History of Marion County, Iowa* . . . (2 vols., Chicago, 1915), 1:181.

[9] The Des Moines Valley R. R., originally the Keokuk, Des Moines & Minnesota R. R., had been completed from Keokuk to Eddyville by 1860. The president of this railroad, Hugh T. Reid, was shortly to be appointed Colonel of the 15th Iowa, and, as such, would incur a good deal of Boyd's wrath—a not unusual dislike of the soldier for his commanding officer. For an account of the Des Moines Valley R. R., see Tacitus Hussey, "How the Des Moines Valley Railroad Came to Des Moines," *Annals of Iowa* (third series), 8:125–34 (July, 1907). For Reid's part in the Civil War, see *Roster Iowa Soldiers*, 2:895; A. A. Stuart, *Iowa Colonels and Regiments* . . . (Des Moines, 1865), 281–8.

on We are told that this comfortable spot is a military Camp and named "Camp Halleck." I do not think much of Mr Halleck if this is a specimen of his Camp I do not wish any farther acquaintance with Mr Halleck

During the night some one brought us some blankets and with some old quilts and a Blanket apiece we got through until morning With husky voices and sore throats we looked around at dawn for something indicating a *change* The only change we met was a breakfast of Bakers bread a little fat bacon and some coffee made in some old rusty kettles The quenchless spirit of liberty which is supposed to exist in limited quantities in volunteers here began to develop and some of the boys began to think of their *mothers* and to talk of returning to their comfortable homes in the western counties This set the officers to working and they went down in the City and when they came back they informed us that we were to be moved to more comfortable quarters Here came in a great *cheer* and we left the Halleck Hotel for down town We marched down Main street by the "Estes House" the largest building I ever saw and take up our abode in a brick building on [the] opposite side of the street from the Estes House and on a corner diagonaly across. The building has several large store rooms in it and under the Sign of Stannus and Co we commence to do business. I think we shall like Stannus and Co better than Mr Halleck. I suppose and hope that Halleck has nothing more to do with us. Our Room is 100 feet long and 25 feet wide The building is full of soldiers and two other companies are in the same room

Our Company is assigned to the 15th Iowa Regiment Volunteers and our Company will be Known as "G" Company Here we commence to have a name But what troubles us most is who shall feed us and wherewith shall we be clothed

Oct 24th Our fears are quieted as regards clothes. We have been required to throw away, give away or otherwise dispose of our citizens dress and we to-day drew from a Quarter-Master down on Johnston street a complete suit of Army blue The clothes we think are very nice and we are as proud as peacocks of our apperance [sic] How we pity those poor miserable fellows at home No new clothes because they will not go soldiering Here we are having lots of fun and glory

To-day we were *sworn* in the service of the United States for three years or during the war Almost every one thinks we will scarcely have a chance to see the enemy as the war will soon end But I guess the government knows more on this subject that we do as it begins to look a little suspicious that we have been *sworn* in for at least three years. We may be going to see all we want to before the row is over But here goes for glory or for fun

The following Muster Roll will show the names and rank of our Company "G" as organized this date and recognized in the 15th Regiment[10]

Muster Roll Co "G" 15th Iowa Infty.

Cunningham Wm T	Capt		18.	Davis John W	"
Hanks Romulus L	1st Lieut		19.	Duncan John [James] W	"
Fisk Hezekiah	2d Lieut		20.	Davis John G	"
Boyd C F	1st Sergt		21.	Derry George W	"
Cathcart William	2d "		22.	Embree W. C.	"
Gray Amos H	3d "		23.	Edmonds William R	"
Welch Josiah M	4th "		24.	Essex Hiram	"
Stanfield Joseph W	5th "		25.	Eldridge Rufus R [H]	"
			26.	Elliott Elisha	"
Clark Mathew	1st Corp		27.	Essex Alexander	"
Myers David	2d "		28.	Ford Oscar	"
Hayes Nathan	3d "		29.	Feagins Granville	"
Hocket Jefferson	4th "		30.	Finn Carl	"
Embree Daniel	6th "		31.	Fisher Daniel	"
McNutt Oliver H	7th "		32.	Glenn Jessee [Jesse] V	"
Shepard Stiles F	8th "		33.	Glenn James W	"
1. Amon Joseph	Private		34.	Gray, John F	"
2. Bunn David H	"		35.	Hooten [Hooton] Henry	"
3. Boothe John F	"		36.	Harger John	"
4. Bidgood William	"		37.	Hannan John	"
5. Brobst Albert	"		38.	Heatley [Heatly] John [James B.]	"
6. Bye E P	"		39.	James William W	"
7. Beebout William H	"		40.	Johnson Thomas J	"
8. Booth John W	"		41.	Judkins Miles	"
9. Campbell William	"		42.	Kerr Levi	"
10. Copeland Samuel	"		43.	Kitchell Wesley	"
11. Carkins Marion	"		44.	Lawhead Alfred	"
12. Crosby Albert N	"		45.	Locker George W	"
13. Chapin James C	"		46.	Morris Harrison	"
14. Cummins George B	"		47.	Mart Marion	"
15. Clark William C	"		48.	Metz Henry	"
16. Creswell Robert J [I]	"		49.	McNeil Alfred	"
17. Clark John W	"				

[10] The spelling of the names has been checked with the roster of the company in *Roster Iowa Soldiers*, 2:895–1055 passim. Corrections are indicated in brackets. In the diary, no Fifth Corporal was listed.

50. McClure Robert M   "   64. Saunders John W   "
51. Metcalf Warren   "   65. Smith Samuel C   "
52. Mullen John   "   66. Stone Truman   "
53. Mayers John   "   67. Swaggart David [Daniel] "
54. Mote William   "   68. Sanders Richard   "
55. McGilvery Alexander   "   69. Sherwood William T   "
56. Netherow David   "   70. Shoemaker Enos   "
57. Nichol[l]s Charles   "   71. Stalcop Mathias   "
58. Owen Henry   "   72. Webb Charles   "
59. Parker William   "   73. Webb John A   "
60. Rid[d]len Timothy   "   74. Welch James L   "
61. Reid Harvey M   "   75. Walker Charles   "
62. Shank Lewis W   "   76. Wyatt H. B.   "
63. Spencer Darwin   "

Thus we stood at the time we were organized 31 of the Company came from Warren County and the balance from Marion County.

Dec. 12th The interval between dates herein has been occupied in company drill and the duties of Camp life which are monotonous enough Taken off the farms as the most of us have been and shut up in a pen as we are is enough to kill the best of us Measles and other diseases have reduced our numbers for drill almost one half and many of the men are sick[11]

We were *sworn* in again to-day by Captain Brown a United States Mustering Officer and now I guess we are *fast* enough We have no arms except a few old muskets which we use in the Manual of Arms up in a hall where the officers drill about three hours every forenoon The orderly sergts are permitted to drill with the Commissioned officers Capt Belknap of the City Guards drill[s] us He is a West Point Graduate and a splendid drill master, and a gentleman in every sense of the word.[12]

[11] Because of lack of adequate medical supplies, often simple diseases caused many deaths among the Union soldiers. Annie Turner Wittenmyer reported on the 15th Iowa in her report of Jan. 13, 1862: "The 15th regiment, now quartered in Keokuk, is suffering severely from measles. The Medical College has been fitted up for hospital purposes, and is pretty well arranged for the accommodation of the sick. There are now 73 in hospital, but most of them are convalescent. The supplies provided by Government being altogether too limited to meet the demands of the sick, the citizens and the Aid Society of this place have generously made up the deficiency. The hospital is visited daily by the ladies, with food and delicacies for the sick. . . ." Keokuk *Weekly Gate City*, Jan. 13, 1862.

[12] William W. Belknap of Keokuk, thirty-two at this time, was a native of New York. He rose rapidly in the service to the rank of Brigadier General in 1864 and

Jany 15th, 1862 I have been up home and to Indianola Had a good time The *girls* all treated me well Brought back with me some recruits as follows:

Boyd Luther S	Cozad John W
Cozad John J	Kerr Thomas
Nichol[l]s William	Mote William
Posegate William [Posegate Francis]	Reid Elias
Safford Thomas	Roberts Samuel

Some of these boys will stand the service and some of them will not. All have to pass through a medical examination But the surgeons are not all particular as the government wants men and these Boys who want to go to war hide all the defects they can There seems to be a great surplus of men now offering and it looks like all that are mustered in now will be all that will be wanted

Brother Scott is determined to go and all I can say to him will not keep him at home Father, Mother, Mary and Jennie left at Home How lonesome it looks there Brother Matt enlisted in April in the 3d Regiment and he is South now The farm at home deserted by every boy in the family and no one but father to look after the stock and other cares Nearly all the boys in the neighborhood are gone *All* in fact who have any ambition in them The towns are almost deserted Every one is talking about the war and crowds throng the Post offices to get the last news.

Feby 22d The space between this and the last date has been passed without any particular change in quarters Many of the men are sick and there are too many of us crowded together in such a small space We were promised a Holiday upon this anniversary provided we appeared respectably at 10 Oclock in Dress Parade Before repairing to the Parade ground we formed in front of our quarters and marched to a nice piece of street on Main and Johnson The Regiment was broken into platoons and the Chap-

was brevetted Major General in 1865. Boyd's statement that he was a graduate of West Point is an error; Belknap had attended Princeton University and had studied law. In Keokuk, where he settled in 1853, he went into partnership with Ralph P. Lowe, future governor of Iowa. After the war Belknap served in Grant's cabinet as Secretary of War for seven years; in 1876 he resigned that post in disgrace, under accusations of official misconduct. He died in Washington in 1890 and is buried in the National Cemetery at Arlington. Benjamin F. Gue, *History of Iowa* . . . (4 vols., New York, 1903), 4:17-18. For Belknap's Civil War record, see *Roster Iowa Soldiers*, 2:895; Stuart, *Iowa Colonels and Regiments* . . ., 289-94.

lain Mr Estabrook [13] an Episcopalian and Lieut Colonel Wm Dewey [14] got upon a stand prepared for the purpose The attention of the Regiment was asked and the Chaplain said the farewell address of Washington would be read The men were called to a "rest" and the Chaplain offered a prayer — or rather read one — Then followed the reading of the address After this Lieut Col Dewey introduced Hugh T Reid by saying "Boys behold your Colonel" and we beheld him The announcement was followed by deafening cheers In a brief speech the Col addressed the Regiment and complimented the men upon their appearance and highly eulogized their conduct since they have been in Keokuk and urged all to follow the noble conduct of the Iowa Regiments that have gone before us. Three cheers were given for Major Belknap who seems to be a favorite — and for the Country Then we marched back to our quarters. . . .

Took dinner and went to the Hospital and saw our sick men Mote and Hooten are very sick and the former will have a hard time to get well The Hospital looks bad for want of proper care The sick are mostly of old and chronic cases of disease I shall not get sick if it can be avoided as I have a holy horror of a Hospital As I came back met some young ladies of recent acquaintance and also saw two drunk men who seemed a little too patriotic for the good of the service They have imbibed too much of the spirit of 76 which seems to be kept in any quantities in the numerous saloons

Corp David Myers and myself went out shooting awhile Attended Dress Parade at 5 oclock Had 56 men out Every man has to go who can walk It is my duty as Orderly Sergt to know whether he can walk or not. I have

[13] William W. Estabrook served as Chaplain of the 15th Iowa until 1863 when he resigned. In May of 1864 he was appointed Surgeon of the 45th Iowa, a "one hundred days" regiment, and was mustered out September 16, 1864. Roster Iowa Soldiers, 2:896; 5:1289.

[14] William Dewey of Sidney, Iowa, a native of Massachusetts, was fifty at the time of his appointment as Lt. Col. of the 15th Iowa. He proved extremely unpopular with the men of the regiment, as will be shown by Boyd's criticisms, and in August, 1862, was transferred to the 23rd Iowa as Colonel; he died in November of that year at Patterson, Mo. Dewey had attended West Point, although he had not been graduated from that institution, and had also studied law and medicine. Captain James G. Day of Co. I, 15th Iowa, later said of him: "He was . . . too irascible and excitable to command respect, or to become a successful leader"; while A. A. Stuart wrote: "He was strict and exacting in his discipline, which did not accord with the democratic notions of his men." James G. Day, "The Fifteenth Iowa at Shiloh," "War Sketches and Incidents . . . Iowa Commandery, Military Order of the Loyal Legion of the United States (2 vols., Des Moines, 1893), 2:176; Stuart, Iowa Colonels and Regiments . . ., 382. See also Roster Iowa Soldiers, 2:895; 3:685.

to call the Roll at breakfast, at dinner and at 8 oclock P M Have to take every man who complains of sickness to Surgeons Call at 9 AM and if excused by the Surgeon he is "off duty" for that day only unless sent to the hospital

Mud deep and growing deeper Uniforms in bad plight — feet wet and cold and patriotism down to zero. After dusk I took a walk up town in the immediate neighborhood of the Catholic Church and stayed until 12 o'clock M As I came back met a drunk soldier on the high side walk near the Church He made a mis-slip and rolled off and down the clay bank clear to the bottom of the gutter I did not stop to enquire if he got his clothes soiled or not. I think the next morning will show that they were not only soiled but *subsoiled* I heard a grave voice at the bottom swearing that it would be "a brick house and forty dollars in money" whatever that may mean Arrived safely at Camp and with the Pass word passed the guard and fell into my bunk

Feby 23d Sunday — The weather is quite warm and damp and the Miss River is beginning to thaw some. Had men in line at 10 AM for Company Inspection This is ordered by Army Regulations Every man must have on his complete uniform except overcoat We have no Arms yet. Only a dozen old muskets for guard duty Company is formed — we open ranks Front rank about faces and at the word of command every man deposits his knapsack on the ground in front of him and opens it for the Inspection of the Captain If a mans clothes are dirty and the articles not properly packed he is reprimanded publicly and told how not to do so next time

The men mostly attended church to-day. I attended Congregational and heard the Rev Mr Thatcher Attended Sunday School at the Exchange M. E. Church and had an interesting time The congregation looked well and I like the place The people are very sociable — especially the young ladies who seem to take a great interest in the soldiers Went to the Hospital in afternoon and visited our sick men Mote and Overton are very sick

Feby 24th Weather cold and disagreeable This forenoon attended officers drill in the large Hall in the Estes House Major Belknap drilled us. All the commissioned officers and the sargts are required to be there promptly Major Belknap is a large lusty and fine looking man and seems to know what he is doing as he puts us through without any resting for about one hour and one half Had Battalion drill in the afternoon Had Dress Parade and thence to supper Sergt Tom Hedrick and I went out calling this eve Called on the Miss Graham's and Miss Lizzie Wiggins and then went up to the Rev Mr Hardeys the ME Minister and spent a pleasant hour

Feby 25th It has been warm enough to-day to leave an overcoat most any place and forget where you put it. Called Roll at Reveille 6 A M Two or three men were in their bunks and did not come out They were slapped on *Extra* duty Went to Post office and detailed guard 1 man on guard, 1 on Police, 1 sergt and 1 man on general guard and 3 men on local police Had Company drill with 64 men out. Our Company now numbers 99 men

Was at Hospital this after noon The sick are getting along as well as we can expect There are many cases of suffering there Some with the Rheumatism seem to be the worst off — for they are completely helpless and suffer great pain Some are used up by the measles and are very low — A young boy who came from Warren County and who enlisted in Co "K" died last night, and this eve another man died from effects of measles.

Went over to Mrs Conrads and saw Dan Embree who has the measles. He has a comfortable place and a good Room — a good bed — good music and seems to enjoy having the measles more than any other one whom I have seen with that disease I almost wish I had postponed having the measles when quite small

Last night the men had high old times running from the Patrol guard Some of them were caught and are now in the "guard house" for several hours or days as the case may be Some of them are getting pretty old at the business of running the guard The Patrol has to do some good running to overtake these night fellows The patrol sometimes find men away from Camp two miles in saloons and disreputable houses There are some bad men in Co's "A & H"

Our Regimental officers are as follows

Hugh T Reid	Colonel
William Dewey	Lieut Colonel
William W. Belknap	Major
George Pomutz	Adjutant
Mortimer A Higley	Qr Master
Jesse Penniman	Sergt Major
William W. Estabrook	Chaplain

Feby 26th Weather mild Have been busy all day. We spend a good deal of time drilling This evening attended a social at a Mr Vails. Waited

on Miss Lizzie Sullivan home Fell down *twice* going back to camp The
streets are terribly rough

Feby 27th Snow storm this morning Took tea at Mrs Conrad's and
heard some good music Dan Embree still lingers there His supply of
measles is holding out well Helped Tom Safford and Cummins to the Hospital to-day Tom is the clown of the Company He will not die as long as
there is any show for *fun* above ground but is not worth a cent for any
other purpose

Feby 28th Weather cool and streets muddy Had Company drill in forenoon and Battalion drill in the afternoon The officers have boarded with
the Company ever since we came here in our quarters until of late They
now board out in town on 3d street. Hanks wants me to go up to his board-
ing place and see the *girls* there He says they are about *right*

Brother Scott has been very sick all day. Spent the evening in quarters
A rumor came to-day that 3000 rebels are in the vicinity of Athens a little
town up the Des Moines river and some men came down from there to get
a cannon for the defence of the place — but I have learned that Camp is no
place for *facts* The River still remains closed and no prospect of its opening
We are watching the ice with no little anxiety as we expect to leave here
[as] soon as boats can run The Spring will open with a vigorous prosecu-
tion of the war and we shall be shoved to the front

March 1st To-day the weather has been drizzling and the sky clouded
Have not been so busy as usual Ten men sick in Company to-day Found
men all improving at hospital Called on the Miss Johnstons[15] this evening
Had a good social time This is w[h]ere Capt and Lieut Hanks board To
night was awful dark I knew because I was out

March 2d Sunday. We had rain, snow and a general amalgamation of
the elements. Attended Church at the Exchange and Sunday School in
afternoon

March 3d Weather extremely cold and windy. More snow to-day This
afternoon have been writing out Discharges for several men who will be
sent home They are sick and already played out The well one's have been
dancing about all day to the music of two or three violins Got up at midnight last night and let a sick man have my bunk in the little back room
where Capt and Lieut sleep

[15] In 1865 Boyd, then a resident of Des Moines, married Miss Maggie Johnston of
Keokuk. Indianola *Weekly Banner*, March 16, 1865.

March 4th   Weather cold and windy. We tried bat[talion] drill this afternoon but it was so cold we did not remain out long Went to a social this evening with Miss Maggie Johnston at a Mr Pattersons on Bank and 7th streets We had a good time and came back about 12 M

March 5th   Did not drill any to-day too cold and windy 14 men off duty to-day in our Company and 2 not expected to live A member of the Company by the name of Locker was arrested for letting things stick to his fingers Capt found a revolver upon him which he lost some time ago Locker was sent to the Guard House

March 6th   Very Muddy. Went down to the shooting gallery with Lieuts Hanks and Fisk and beat them both shooting at a target 30 yards Have dress parade as usual every evening At Parade this eve there was presented to the view of the Reg't the flag of the 2d Iowa which was carried over the defences of Fort Donelson which place was captured a few days ago with a great number of prisoners The flag was held up by a wounded soldier of the 2d The sight called forth a great cheer from all the men There was a large quantity of the arms captured at Donelson sent here for exhibition — such as old muskets, Arkansaw "tooth-picks" &c Also some fragments of a shell which exploded in the gun boat Essex and killed 30 men. . . .[16]

March 8th   The River is thawing and there is a good prospect of its opening soon Called at the Johnston residence this evening and spent an hour very pleasantly — also visited an hour at Mrs Hanfords in same way.

March 9th Sunday — I attended Unitarian Church to-day and heard Rev Mr Whitney preach. His subject was the War and its Cause. It was a good sermon He said that human slavery was the Cause and we should have no lasting peace until the Curse was wiped out Took dinner at Mr Johnstons and had a pleasant stay afterwards. Remained in quarters this eve and wrote some letters

March 10th   Weather beautiful. Had Bat. drill Major Belknap commanded the left wing to which our Co belongs Tie Shephard and *me self* went up to see the Sullivan family (only a part of it) this evening Lizzies family are full blooded Irish and the old gent['s] nose turns up just like a

---

[16] For an account of the part played by the 2nd Iowa at Fort Donelson, see Mildred Throne (ed.), "The Civil War Diary of John Mackley," IOWA JOURNAL OF HISTORY, 48:163-4 (April, 1950). An "Arkansas toothpick" was a knife similar to a bowie knife. Mitford M. Matthews (ed.), *A Dictionary of Americanisms* . . . (2 vols., Chicago, 1951), 1:42.

true son of Cork The old lady is a clever sly little woman and very shy
Lizzie is a fast talker and her eyes are sparkling black and as sharp as any
Irish girl She has an independent air which makes her entertaining and she
does not seem to care whether School keeps or not In our rambles we did
not reach camp until about 12 oclock We saw the patrol guard chasing
some fellow down 5th street and up Johnston and finaly [sic] caught him
He was taken to the guard house there to suffer the penalty of his crime.

March 11th Fine weather just now and the River thawing rapidly I
want this river to thaw out and again I do *not* We are drilling in foot
maneuvers

March 12th Gloriously cold and windy News came to-day that the
Rebs have evacuated Manassas. Gen Curtis has whipped the combined
forces of Price, Van Dorn and McIntosh at Pea Ridge in Arkansas.[17] Our
troops seem to be gaining signal victories every place Almost every one
thinks the war will end soon

Dave Myers and I called at Mr Johnstons this eve It looks a little as if I
was going to Mr Johnstons rather often Some of the up town girls have
made the above remark in my *hearing* lately They may be correct

March 13th Weather cloudy with high wind The River commenced
breaking up this afternoon and the ice is piling up in large islands on the
bars and shallow places The main guard having been taken off for a few
days was again put on duty to-day. There was considerable profane language used about it by the men

This evening *Sergt* Dave Myers (recently promoted from Corporal) took
Miss Aggie and I escorted Miss Maggie Johnston to call on a Miss Ella
Creel who lives on 7th Street. While we were there it commenced to rain
and when we came back the pavements were in a terribly slippery condition
When we got back to quarters the guard halted us — and we continued to
halt The guard remained silent and we enquired what *next* Not answering
we asked him if he wanted the countersign and he said he *believed* he did
We advanced and whispered in his *dirty ear* "Pea Ridge" He than had
presence of mind enough to tell us to Pass on This fellow was perhaps on
guard for the first time But it was not the first time *out* for us

[17] General Samuel Ryan Curtis of Keokuk, first Colonel of the 2nd Iowa, had been
placed in command of the District of Southwest Missouri in December, 1861. For an
account of the battle of Pea Ridge, which cleared Arkansas of Confederate troops,
see Stuart, *Jowa Colonels and Regiments* . . ., 38–44.

March 14th Weather cool Ice almost all gone out of the River at this place, and the water is rising fast Last night a hard rain fell Rumor says that we shall leave soon for the South. I hope we will for it is getting too muddy and many of the men are getting sick Our quarters are crowded and damp. 14 men off duty today in Co

March 15th Weather cloudy and damp. The ice is gathering in large drifts below town The gorge rests at Alexandria Have been busy all day getting Company concerns ready to leave. We are drawing clothing and complete equipments except arms Took supper with Tie Shepard at the "Wiggins House" by special invitation of Miss Lizzie W.

March 16th Sunday Weather beautiful Went to Exchange to Church and [heard] "Uncle" John Cozad preach He is past 50 years of age. Is a full blooded "democrat" and came with me from Indianola He had to resort to strategy to get in the service He had his hair colored black — held his head up and looked like a boy under age — and ran the gauntlet of Inspection and was sworn in Company "G" as a private soldier[18] He wants to go principaly [sic] because his *son* John has enlisted in our Company at the age of 17 and he is an only child and the poor old man cannot bear to have him go alone so he goes along to look after him Went to Sunday School in the afternoon and saw several of the young ladies In the evening attended church at the O. S. P. with Miss Maggie J.

March 17th Everybody is excited We received orders to prepare to leave Keokuk To draw three days rations and to be ready at a moments notice to embark. Destination unknown Extra Cooks were detailed and things are being hurried on This afternoon some of us went around and bid good-bye to some of our lady friends Perhaps we will have to do this over again as the prospect this evening is that we shall not go for some days yet But then if we should remain awhile it will not hurt us much to — as we should just as soon see some of them again as not Went to a Concert this eve and took a lady friend

March 18th Weather cloudy and wet. If certain boats come up tonight we shall leave to-morrow Have been very busy all day This afternoon we

[18] According to the army records, John J. Cozad of Indianola was forty-four years old at the time of his enlistment, but he had been born in Ohio in 1812, which indicates that he age he gave the mustering officer was incorrect by some six years. He had been rejected by the 10th Iowa, but had succeeded in being accepted by the 15th. He served until Feb., 1863, when he was discharged for "general disability." *Roster Iowa Soldiers,* 2:175, 922; *History of Warren County* . . ., 620.

marched with Knapsacks on We find that we shall have a mules load to carry — 2 blankets, extra clothing and a big overcoat, haversack &c saying nothing about a gun and ammunition

Tie Shepard and I took tea with Miss Lizzie Sullivan Miss Hart was there and we had a good time Never were men treated so well as we have been by the good people of Keokuk They have all seemed to study the interests and the happiness of the soldiers and have provided every comfort that can be imagined They have used us too well and we will suffer for it when we leave here Came past the Miss Grahams and bid them good-bye The Johnston girls gave us some ginger snaps and I have my haversack full of provisions

Miss River — on board the "Jennie Deans"

March 19th This morning our quarters presented a busy scene Many of the men were up at 3 o'clock getting ready to fly from this old Nest The boat "Jennie Deans" came up and we were to leave at 3 PM Two or three of us took dinner with the Johnston girls Maggie and Aggie We had a good dinner and a pleasant time not unmarred however by the ever present thought that this might be the *last* time we should meet these kind people With many kind wishes for our safety and welfare we bid them good-bye When we returned to Quarters we found the men ready to march to the landing and with one last lingering look at the old bunks we bid them a final and last farewell

The rain was falling in torrents as we marched down Main street But notwithstanding this all the side walks were crowded with people All the windows were full of women and children waving flags and handkerchiefs The sick boys at the Hospital looked out from their bunks to cast a glance at the long line of blue with its glistening knapsacks with its steady march to the music by the bands of "Dixies Land" 1000 strong we marched that afternoon in the pride and glory of youthful soldiers The sound of the music — the cheering shouts of the people robbed [us] of all regrets and we marched proudly away. I saw some of our good friends on the side walks — but it would not do to look back We were marched on board the "Jennie Deans" and crowded like cattle into every conceivable corner No man unless he wears shoulder straps can enter the cabin When the boat left shore thousands of people stood upon the wharf and cheer after cheer arose as we turned to the South and glided into the stream

The whole face of the River was covered with cakes of ice As darkness

came on many of the men went below and found room to lie down I found
a sheltered place near one of the chimnies on the upper deck and spread my
blanket and slept soundly for about two hours when the cold wind awakened me and I got up and not seeing any guard at the cabin door I crept in
and laid down on the floor

"Benton Barracks" St Louis

March 20th Got up at 5 oclock this morning Soon after daylight we
passed Alton Ills and by 9 AM we were at the landing in St Louis among a
perfect mass of steam boats which lay along the shore as far as the eye
could reach We were ordered to land and soon were on the march to Benton Barracks, which is four or five miles out. The streets were muddy and
slippery and many weak men gave out on this our first march We were
kept on the double quick most of the time and most of us were gone up
when we got to the Barracks. After two hours standing and stumbling
around our officers apportioned each Company its place in the barracks.
The quarters are comfortable and convenient and the boys have so far re-
covered as to have a *dance* to-night The people cheered us from almost
every house as we came out and waved flags and rags Now we shall learn
something of the Art of War

March 21st Snowed about all day and melted as fast as it fell making it
awful muddy A battery of art[illery] arrived to-day from Camp Denison
Ohio consisting of six field pieces and 136 men Capt P Gad Bryan of the
1st Iowa Cav arrived here to-day on his way to his Regiment.

March 22d This has been a cool and windy day until evening when the
sun came out and dried some of the mud. Many of the troops located here
were out drilling this afternoon But the 15th did nothing in that line 17th
Wisconsin came in to-day all armed and equiped [sic] — they march well
and looked splendidly The 16th Iowa came in from Dubuque last night,
1000 strong

I took a ramble around the barracks to-day to see some of the preparations making for the organization of the Western Army The Headquarters
of this encampment consists of a large three story building — frame and
built square and a large flag floats over the house The soldiers barracks
extend on either side in compact one story frame buildings and string out
about one mile in length on either side of the drill grounds leaving a beautiful piece of ground half a mile in width All the quarters front on this
parade ground Back of these buildings are the kitchens and out houses.

Water is conducted through pipes and can be drawn in any of the Kitchens Underground drains carry off all the refuse water The water for the supply comes from the Miss river Long lines of stables extend back of the Kitchens These are occupied by the Cavalry Here we can begin to see — and to have some idea of the preparations being made to prosecute this War

Saw the 14th Wis Infantry encamped on the Fair grounds in bell — or Sibley tents[19] — They are a fine collection of Men They are packing up this eve preparatory to leaving as also the 23 Mo I saw 33 pieces of Art. to-day Rumor says we shall be sent to New Mexico It takes 136 men for camp guard around the Barracks The who[le] thing is surrounded by a high board fence and Cavalry outside of that

March 23d Sunday Weather cool and some snow fell. There was some movements of troops to-day. Another battery came in last night. There was preaching at the fair grounds to-day but I did not find it out in time to go. There was a great parade of troops There seems to be no Sunday here There seems to be no God here but more than the average amount of Devil Saw a Cavalryman thrown from his horse and badly hurt. One man had his neck broken yesterday

March 24th This has been a fine day and we have improved it by drilling A number of the 17th Wis got drunk to-day and the officers had a great time to manage them News comes of a severe battle at Winchester Va in which our side was victorious

Men selling "bullet proof" vests were in camp to-day The boys say our Capt purchased one They submitted some for trial about one half of them were bored through by musket balls They sold for $8.00 to $16.00 If the bullet did not go through it would knock a man into the middle of next week so that he might as well be killed first as last

March 25th Weather clear and fine Have been busy all day drilling Lieut Fisk has been appointed Asst Surgeon of the Reg't and will be away from the Co most of the time We just begin to like him. His eyes are very

---

[19] The Sibley tent, named for its inventor, "was a cone sixteen feet in diameter at the base, supported by a center pole with an iron tripod foot. The top of the pole supported an iron ring one foot in diameter over which was draped a conical cape which was raised for ventilation and to let out the smoke. Sixteen men occupied each of these tents and slept as radii of the circle with their feet toward the center, where a fire could be built when necessary. . . ." Fred Albert Shannon, *The Organization and Administration of the Union Army, 1861–1865* (2 vols., Cleveland, 1928), 1:200.

sore and he can scarcely see anything Our officers all seem very kind The 65th Ills Infantry went down the River to-day — also one troop of Cavalry.

March 26th Weather clear warm and fine I have to travel one mile to deliver my morning Report and half a mile to Surgeons Call with all the sick who are able to walk and same distance to Post Office This afternoon we drew our Arms — they are Springfield Rifle Muskets and are a most beautiful weapon — they are bright and in fine condition We brought them with all the accouterments to camp and distributed them and every man will be held responsible for everything he drew These guns are effective at from 500 to 800 yards and load with cartridge minnie ball Received to-day by each Company one wagon and six mules to haul Company baggage.

March 27th Weather warmest of the season Have all been attacked with spring-fever or symptoms to that effect. Have drilled in the manual of Arms to-day and here we show our greeness [sic] Received a letter from Home The scenes around these old barracks are becoming so common that we want another change

March 28th Weather warm and we had a fine little thunder shower this afternoon — 11th Ills Cav left to-day for some unknown destination We received *Marching orders* this evening On hearing this the men cheered for about half an hour so anxious are they to go The order was announced on dress parade

March 29th A good day for spring fever and it took hold of a good many. Have been busy all day preparing to leave for the South This eve the 15th Mich came in tired, dirty and used up The Regt numbers about 900 and are armed with Austrian muskets a very clumsy looking Gun

March 30th Sunday The air to-day has been refreshingly cool and the sky clear and the sun shone out brightly There is Sunday in the almanac but in military affairs there seems to be no sacred day All is work. The men are playing cards swearing and dancing just as on other days. This I do not enjoy How uncomfortable it makes me to be thus surrounded on Sunday Through the week I can get along very well Men that four months ago would not use a profane word can now outswear many others and those who would even shun a checker board now play cards for profit The descent looks gradual from the top but how fast they seem to go as everything seems to hurry on the downward grade If the war should last a year or two how degraded some of these men will become How eager they seem to abandon all their early teachings and to catch up with everything which tends to debase To-day each Company has been cooking rations for the trip ahead Officers have been making Muster Rolls

March 31st Have been very busy all day Expect to start to-morrow morning

"Toward Dixies Land" Steamer Minnehaha

April 1st We arose at 4 O'clock and expected to leave at 7 O'clock — but we did not get off until 11 A M Our Regiment with the 16th Iowa, 23d Missouri and 15th Mich came down together to the landing — all armed and equipped with the bands all playing They looked fine and gay indeed We went aboard the steamboat "Minnehaha" and after two hours of tedious waiting started down the stream toward "Dixies" land The other boats did not start when we did We had aboard also two Batteries and all the horses belonging thereto and our Regimental wagons

The "Minnehaha" is an old shaky tub and is very large Every available place and corner is crowded — Around the boilers the men are packed like swine We ran aground this evening and the shock brought everything up *standing* and frightened many of the men for a moment After the boat got off she ran a short distance and threw out her anchor close to an Island I shall sleep just in the rear of one of the wheel houses in a little spot marked out by my knapsack and gun &c

April 2d This morning about 4 O'clock the steamer again started and kept bravely on her course down the river We have made our first attack upon *"hard tack"* this morning and think we shall like it We have bid fare-well to Bakers bread, cows milk and such soft things. Had a piece of meat and a hard tack for breakfast — we are gradualy breaking in The scenery along the river is very picturesque and beautiful especially on the Ills side High rocky cliffs covered with Cedar in many places There is always a contrast when one side is rough and hilly the other side will be flat and swampy

This afternoon we stop[p]ed at Cape Girardeau on the Mo side The town is situated on steep and high hills On the summit of the highest hill in the town is a large fort made of earth from which a piece of artillery was fired as we came almost opposite and then our boat rounded to and came to land-ing We remained only a few minutes Saw a few soldiers on shore. There seems to be quite a number of pieces of artillery here The town is built mostly of brick The wind being high the waves splashed upon the deck and frightened the mules and horses

This afternoon one of the rudder ropes broke and we drifted for some time with the current At 5 o'clock PM we came in sight of Cairo lying at the mouth of the Ohio river On the West side of the Miss is Birds Point a somewhat noted place of late It is a low flat piece of land and seems to be covered with timber Cairo lies in a low muddy piece of ground just at the junction of the Ohio and Miss rivers and is a most forbidding looking place The levee hides from river view the most of the town. Some of the houses stand in water to the first windows — the inmates living in the upper stories They have small Canoes and paddle from one house to the other No "swinging on the gates" allowed here A long line of Boats lie along the Ohio wharf. I think the principal productions of Cairo are tad-poles and ague "Fort Holt" lies on the Kentucky side among the heavy timber which hides from view the adjacent country — Distance from St Louis 180 miles Sixteenth Iowa came down this eve. Weather clear & warm

April 3d Went on shore and made some coffee this morning — which never tasted so good — and it cheered us up Left Cairo at 8 O'clock Kept up the Ohio and most of the time close to the Kentucky shore Passed a beautiful little village almost hid among the newly budding trees and green blue grass The people cheered loudly as we passed On the North or Ills side the country is rough and on the other side the opposite while the high water is flooding the low lands.

At 5 O'clock we came to Paducah Kentucky — a mean dirty looking town with its low black brick walls and old smoky buildings — lying just at the junction of the Tennessee river and on the west bank Here are plenty of soldiers and several boat loads of old muskets and spoils of war brought down from Donelson and Henry[20] The river bank is lined with soldiers and dirty greasy negroes We have tied up at the shore and will remain here until morning Paducah is a *secession* town and came near being taken by General Simon Buckner at one time but the vigilance of Gen. Grant seemed the point which is of great importance About 8000 troops are here

April 4th To-day we have been at anchor expecting every moment to leave but did not get away until 4 PM We left with other boats and all the bands playing "Dixies" Land Here we enter the dark land of secession and the enemies home Kentucky professes to be *neutral* which means that she leans heavily toward secession She takes this ground only to save her own

[20] The battles of Forts Henry and Donelson had taken place on February 6 and 15, 1862.

hide — but she will strike us a blow soon as she thinks we cannot strike back Met the Gunboat "Cairo" a formidable looking vessel — she carries 12 heavy guns — some of them 68 pounders

April 5th Last night we traveled until 11 o'clock and a storm coming on we hauled into shore and remained until 4 o'clock this morning The rain drove the men below and we were desperately crowded for room. Passed Fort Henry about 4 o'clock The fort is occupied by a small garrison Fort Donelson is a short distance away on the Cumberland river — Henry seems to have been a strong place for Riflemen but could not stand the fire of heavy art. from the gunboats which produced such a panic among the "secesh" that they retired to Fort Donelson where they were all taken in by Genl Grant

Battle of Shiloh or Pittsburgh Landing [21]

April 6th Sunday — At 6 o'clock we arrived at a point known as "Pittsburgh Landing" on the West bank of the Tenn river where seems to be concentrated all the western troops that are destined to invade the Confederacy by way of the Mississippi Valley This place is 240 miles from the mouth of the Tennessee river At 7 o'clock we ate breakfast on board the

[21] In the Battle of Shiloh, or Pittsburg Landing, the 2nd, 3rd, 6th, 7th, 8th, 11th, 12th, 13th, 14th, 15th, and 16th Iowa Regiments took part. Colonel Wm. T. Shaw of the 14th called it "Iowa's great battle of the Rebellion." See Wm. T. Shaw, "The Battle of Shiloh," *War Sketches and Incidents* . . ., 1:183-4. Much has been written about the battle of Shiloh; endless controversy resulted as to whether Grant was caught napping when the Confederate army, under the command of General Albert Sidney Johnston, moved out of Corinth and attacked suddenly on the morning of April 6. For Grant's own account, see *Personal Memoirs of U. S. Grant* (2 vols., New York, 1885), 1:330-70. Some other accounts are: Joseph W. Rich, *The Battle of Shiloh* (Iowa City, 1911); Henry Stone, "The Battle of Shiloh," and Ephraim C. Dawes, "The Battle of Shiloh," in *Campaigns in Kentucky and Tennessee* . . . (Vol. VII of *Papers of the Military Historical Society of Massachusetts*, Boston, 1908), 33–202; D. C. Buell, "Shiloh Reviewed," *Century Magazine*, 31:749–81 (March, 1886); S. H. M. Byers, *Iowa in War Times* (Des Moines, 1888), 122–45; S. D. Thompson, *Recollections with the Third Iowa Regiment* (Cincinnati, 1864), 206–256; Clinton Parkhurst, "A Few Martial Memories [of the 16th Iowa at Shiloh]," *The Palimpsest*, 1:111–28 (October, 1920); Henry Steele Commager (ed.), *The Blue and the Gray* . . . (2 vols., Indianapolis, 1950), 1:351–5; Otto Eisenschiml and Ralph Newman, *The American Iliad* . . . (Indianapolis, 1947), 168–203; *The War of the Rebellion: A Compilation of the Official Records of the Union and Confederate Armies* . . ., Series I, Vol. X, Parts I and II, *passim*. (Hereafter referred to as *Official Records*). Pittsburg was a steamboat landing on the Tennessee River in southern Tennessee near the Mississippi border. The battle fought there became known later as "Shiloh" because of Shiloh Church, two miles southwest of the Landing, where General W. T. Sherman's headquarters were located.

Minnehaha at which time we could hear the noise of *cannon*[22] About 9
O'clock brother Matt of the 3d Iowa came in. I of course was glad to see
him His regiment has been out on the front some days. He looks hearty
and well

About this time rumor came that the Rebel General Beauregard[23] with a
large force has attacked our Pickets who are being driven back. The men
of the 3d say it does not mean anything as the firing is of daily occurrence
and is only the pickets At 9 o'clock the wounded began to come in and
there begins to be a great stir on the shore Officers and cavalry riding in
all directions The roar of the cannon can be distinctly heard some miles to
the South

At 10 o'clock we are ordered ashore with all our equipments including
40 rounds of ammunition[24] With our knapsacks haversacks canteen (and
almost every one had an extra suit of clothes) and our overcoats — haversacks filled to the top with hard tack and last but not least each of us had a
big high hat with a large brass "eagle" on the side. If we were not a choice
looking lot of fighting cocks as we stood in line that morning then I am no
guesser We formed in line on the Bluff overlooking the river — We were
in great confusion as Col Reid and Dewey galloped back and forth without
seeming to know exactly what they were doing Col Dewey did a consider-

22 The battle had been joined in earnest between 5 and 6 o'clock in the morning
against the Sixth Division, under command of General B. M. Prentiss. Colonel Reid
of the 15th, in his report later, wrote: ". . . the Fifteenth Regiment of Iowa Volunteer Infantry from Benton Barracks at Pittsburg on Sunday morning, with
orders from General Grant's headquarters to report to General Prentiss. Finding that
his headquarters were some 4 miles from the Landing, I proceeded at once to report
to him in person, and found a heavy fire of artillery and musketry already commenced along his lines. Orders were received from his aide to bring up my command
as soon as possible, and I returned to the river for that purpose." *Official Records*,
Series I, Vol. X, Part I, 278, 288.

23 General A. S. Johnston, in command of the Confederate forces, was killed in the
early afternoon of April 6 and his place taken by General P. G. T. Beauregard. For
descriptions of Johnston's death, see Eisenschiml and Newman, *American Iliad* . . .,
186; William Preston Johnson, "Albert Sidney Johnston and the Shiloh Campaign,"
Century Magazine, 29:621 (February, 1885); Joseph W. Rich, "The Death of General
Albert Sidney Johnston on the Battlefield of Shiloh," IOWA JOURNAL OF HISTORY AND
POLITICS, 16:275–81 (April, 1918).

24 "The regiment was rapidly disembarked, ammunition was distributed, and the
men for the first time loaded their guns," reported Colonel Reid. Thus, green troops
who had only received their rifles some ten days before (March 26) were thrown into
one of the bloodiest battles of the Civil War. *Official Records*, Series I, Vol. X, Part
I, 288.

able amount of hard *swearing* and I had time to notice him wheel his horse around and take some *consolation* through the neck of a pint bottle. This seemed to give him a stronger flow of swear language than before When we had got into something like a line we were presented with several boxes of ammunition and each man ordered to fill up to the extent of 100 rounds By this time we were loaded down to the "guards"

The wounded men were by this time coming in freely and were being carried right through our ranks. And we could see hundreds of soldiers running through the woods. Col Reid got us started Who gave the order I know not Who our guide was I knew not We started on the double quick in the direction of the heavy firing which was mostly of musketry. The field officers were mounted on horses and we tried to keep up with them and to do it we had to *run* and then the front (for the Regt was marching by the right flank) would halt and the rear would telescope into them Thus we kept on for at least three miles meeting hundreds — yes thousands of men on the retreat who had thrown away their arms and were rushing toward the Landing — most of these were *hatless* and had nothing on them except their clothes Some of them were wounded and covered with blood from head to foot Some of the wounded were being carried on stretchers The woods were full of Infantry, cavalry, Artillery and all arms of the service were flying toward the River in countless numbers Men yelled as they passed us "Don't go out there" "You'll catch hell" "We are all cut to pieces" "We are whipped" Some declared they were the only one's left out of a whole Regiment or a Battery as the case may be

There was also Infantry officers with swords drawn and trying to head off the flying troops and make them halt There was Cavalrymen galloping after men and threatening to shoot them if they did not *stop* But I saw no one stop — But on we went facing all these discouraging circumstances to take our turn at failure to stop the Rebel tide which was coming in like a wave of the sea unresisted and irresistable

Here we were a new Regt which had never until this morning heard an enemies gun fire thrown into this *hell* of battle — without warning The hot sun and the dreadful load we had carried through three miles of dust and battle smoke had so exhausted us that there was no strength left in the men. On the bluff we have put the first cartridges into our guns and [that] added to the scenes through which we had just passed was enough to unnerve the best troops in the world But we were *green* and went in and not a man was seen to halt or to falter Lieut Fisk had been in a dark state room all the trip on account of his eyes — but when we formed at the landing he came off the boat and in full uniform insisted on going into the fight. He wanted to take his place as Lieut. Several of us earnestly tried to persuade him to stay out but he would not listen to us and go he did. He was almost blind and followed us to the field

The roar of the artillery and the crash of the musketry was close at hand We came to the edge of a large field and as we crossed a little Ravine the bullets and a few shells passed over us making some of us dodge Here we deployed by the right flank to come into line of battle but did not get that accomplished until we were out in the open field and in fair view of the enemy. A heavy shower of bullets riddled the ranks and threw us into some *more* confusion and being jamed into masses we were in poor shape to return the fire — some were wounded and a few killed before we could come to a front. Here I noticed the first man shot. He belonged in Co "K" Capt Hedricks Co [John M. Hedrick, of Ottumwa] He was close to us and sprang high in the air and gave one groan and fell *dead* Our Company had to pass over him and each man as he came up seemed to hesitate and some made a motion to pick him up — but the officers sternly ordered them "forward" The men all gave a cheer and rushed on in line of battle with bayonets fixed

The enemy lay in ambush at the farther side of the field We at first could not see them only the puffs of white smoke came from the thickets and brush and every log and tree. We reached some scattering trees and [as] if by common consent we made for those and it was fun to see two or three fellows running for the same tree. In the smoke and confusion I saw the flag advancing on our right and running across an open space I made for a small sapling not more than six or eight inches through. When I got there two other fellows were there too and Jeff Hocket was one of them Jeff gave me a tremendous *butt* and sent me out of shelter and displaced me so that the tree was of no use to me We all three laughed and the other fellow and I started for another tree and kept shooting toward the enemy I found a very good place behind a good sized log just to the left with Co "B" and had some good shots from there in the direction of the enemy but could not see them for the smoke There was a little Ravine where Co "B" was working and this protected us from grape and cannister which was being opened in the Regiment from the timber in our front It was every man for himself

We knew nothing about orders or officers Indeed the Companies now became all mixed up and without organization [25]

Col Reid was wounded and fell from his horse with a bullet wound in the neck — Lieut Col Dewey I notice sitting behind a tree holding the halter to his horse which seemed to be badly wounded Major Belknap was wounded and also Adjt Pomutz Sergt Major Penniman had been killed The wounded and the dead lay thickly on the ground

Lieut Rogers of Co "E" had the flag and bore it manfully ahead of all He made one stand behind the upturned roots of.an old tree A heavy fire seemed to be concentrated on the flag and men fell thick all around that spot The enemy opened on us with artillery at close range using grape, canister and shell and all manner of deadly missiles Above the roar of the guns could be heard the cheers of our men as they gained new ground At last we could see the enemy and they were advancing around our left flank and the woods seemed alive with *gray coats* and their victorious cheer and unearthly *yells* and the concentrated fire which they had upon us caused somebody to give the order for *retreat* The word was passed along — and we went off that bloody ground in great confusion and had to fall back over the same open ground by which we came [26]

As we started down the Ravine a wounded rebel caught me by the leg as I was passing and looking up at me said My friend for God's sake give me a *drink* of water He had been shot about the head and was covered with blood to his feet. I at once thought of that command "If thine enemy thirst give him drink" and I halted and tried to get my canteen from under my accouterments — but I could not and pulled away from him and said "I

---

[25] Andrew Hickenlooper, an Ohio officer, wrote: "There were no battle plans, no strategy, no tactical maneuvers and but few commands—certainly none that had any important bearing upon the final results. It was under such conditions that these men —many of whom had never before heard a hostile gun fired—were suddenly aroused and hastily formed in line, without food, without water or even without an adequate supply of ammunition, and were moved forward until suddenly confronted by the regiments of a vigorously pressing and determined foe." Eisenschiml and Newman, *American Iliad . . .*, 203.

[26] "While I admit that after fighting nearly two hours in a regiment 'as green as a gourd,' and losing on the field nearly two hundred gallant men, killed and wounded, I with all others in sight left with some celerity for a more healthy spot; yet we had plenty of company from other regiments and commands, and as far as I saw, the fact that officers of rank were separated from their commands was the rule and not exception. . . ." William W. Belknap, "The Obedience and Courage of the Private Soldier . . .," *War Sketches and Incidents . . .*, 1:160.

have not time to help you" (I had business other places just about that time as the Regt was ahead of me) And on we went making as good time as we ever made over that old field

The bullets seemed to fill the air and to be clipping every little weed and bush and blade of grass around us Many men lost their *hats* and their guns — The tall gov't hats with the glorious old "eagle" lay thick on the ground and the knapsacks and haversacks and last winters overcoats were too numerous to mention

In the meantime (and just about as *mean a time* as I have ever met) the enemies Cavalry came dashing around on our right flank (as we retreated) and followed us almost to the ravine where we made a temporary stand and with a few shots the Cav fell back Here Jeff Hocket ran to me and said that my brother Scott had given out and was lying upon the ground some distance back. I ran to him and tried to get him upon his feet But he said I should go on as he never could go any farther and that I had better save myself and let him go. I told him the enemy were almost upon him and that he would be taken prisoner or killed No words of mine seemed to have any effect I now took him by the *nap of the neck* and jerked him upon his feet and told him to *come* or I should help him with my *boot* At this he stood up and I managed to work him along down the ravine and left him to rally on the hill. The men kept on to the rear and were fast filling up the great stream of *fugitives* from the battle field

Cavalrymen were riding in all directions with drawn sabers and revolvers threatening to shoot and "Cut mens heads off" if they did not stop and rally Officers were coaxing praying and exhorting men for "God's sake" to stop and all make a stand together But in most cases their orders and appeals were not heard by these demoralized men who kept going like a flock of sheep All the terrors of hell would not have stoped them until they got to the River Hundreds lay in the woods on the ground completely overcome with the heat smoke and dust and fatigue The heat seemed intense The air was filled with dense smoke and fumes from burning powder took all the moisture from the mouth and a *burning dryness* extended to the throat

Riderless horses came thundering through the woods with empty saddles and artillery horses with caisons [sic] attached ran through the squads of men and striking trees caused the percussion shells to explode blowing horses caisons and everything around to atoms Cannon balls were flying in all directions cutting off great limbs of trees and many men were killed and injured in this way as the heavy limbs fell on them Every indication seemed to point to a great and *terrible defeat* There seemed to be only a few who thought we were not *whipped*

At this time about 2 o'clock in the afternoon the remains of several Regiments concentrated with our squad under command of Capt Kittle Co "A" with some Ohio Wis and Indiana troops we went forward again toward the line of battle which seemed to have advanced some distance Our Reg flag was carried by Sergt Rogers We kept advancing and falling back as the enemy pressed forward or gave way under heavy fire from troops on our left Our men dragged some heavy guns back of us and the whole line of Infantry fell back and massed around the Artillery

About this time some prisoners brought in say that Albert Sidney Johnston commanding the Rebel army was killed this afternoon and that Beauregard is now in command and has sworn to "water his horse in the Tennessee River or in *hell* before night"

About 5 o'clock the enemy came on in solid masses for the final *charge* At this time there was a calm The artillery and the musketry almost ceased and the calmness was *oppressive* But it was the calm before the terrible *storm* which was preparing We were massed upon the surrounding bluffs about the landing General Grant and Genl Buell rode along the line and urged every man to stand *firm* as we should have thousands of reenforcements in a short time and pointed to the opposite side of the river where we could see a long line of blue coats far as the eye could reach — and that was *Buells Army This sight was all that saved Grants Army*[27] No prom-

---

[27] Maj. Gen. Don Carlos Buell, in command of the Army of the Ohio, had been ordered from Columbia, Tenn., to join Grant at Savannah, a few miles up the river from Pittsburg Landing. He had arrived there with his first division on the evening of April 5, the other divisions following at 6-mile intervals. By the evening of April 6 his Army had been moved up to Pittsburg Landing. *Official Records*, Series I, Vol. X, Part I, 291-2; Buell, "Shiloh Reviewed," 751-2. Jesse Bowen Young, a Union soldier, also drew inspiration from the sight of Buell's army: "Late in the afternoon I noticed a commotion on the other side of the river. Transports were there waiting for something or somebody. As I watched the spot, I saw a squad of men appear in sight on that side of the river. Then came a general and staff, and then on a run a regiment with its battle flags floating gaily in the air. They quickly embarked on transports and in a short time were on the Pittsburg Landing shore. I could hardly believe my eyes as I saw the advance guard and realized that Buell's troops had come to the rescue of the Army of the Tennessee. The arriving troops cheered and were cheered in return. . . ." Eisenschiml and Newman, *American Iliad* . . ., 191.

ises or words could have inspired men on this desperate occasion Every man who stood in that crumbling wall felt the great responsibility. To give way then would be *destruction* to the whole Army

There is some talk now that the enemy having lost their leader is retreating and that the battle is over for to-day which is the reason for the silence But this delusion is soon dissipated as the smoke clears away we can see the enemy coming on in long dark lines and seem to spring out of the ground in countless thousands This is to be the grand and final charge by which they hope to sweep us from the face of the earth or capture the entire army This *death like stillness* is worse than *murder* Our Artillery opens with about 40 pieces (all we have left) then nothing more can be seen

The very earth trembles with the fearful explosions The enemy charged to the very mouth of our cannon and hundreds of them fell — filled with whiskey and gun powder The battle raged for the possession of this hill which we held If we would have lost this *all would have been lost* Every man seemed nerved beyond human strength to do his utmost and he *did.* Acres of dead and wounded told the fearful tale of sacrifice.

At this time two gunboats moved up the River and opened on the flank of the enemy such terrific noises were never before heard in these dismal woods.[28] The rapidity of the discharges and the roar of the guns seemed to mow the very forest to the ground This so demoralized the Rebels that they fell back about dark At this time a grand stampede took place at the Landing

Thousands of men who had fled from the field tried to get aboard the steamboats which lay at the bank The Boats were ordered to leave and fall over to the other bank of the River The crazy fugitives from behind crowded those in front and hundreds were pushed into the River and scores

[28] "At a late hour in the afternoon a desperate effort was made by the enemy to turn our left and get possession of the Landing, transports, &c. This point was guarded by the gunboats Tyler and Lexington, Captains Gwin and Shirk, U. S. Navy, commanding, four 20-pounder Parrott guns and a battery of rifled guns. As there is a deep and impassable ravine for artillery or cavalry, and very difficult for infantry, at this point, no troops were stationed here, except the necessary artillerists and a small infantry force for their support. Just at this moment the advance of Major-General Buell's column (a part of the division under General Nelson) arrived, the two generals named both being present. An advance was immediately made upon the point of attack and the enemy soon driven back. In this repulse much is due to the presence of the gunboats Tyler and Lexington, and their able commanders, Captains Gwin and Shirk." Report of U. S. Grant, April 9, 1862, *Official Records*, Series I, Vol. X, Part I, 109.

drowned The cannon balls from the enemies batteries now passed over our heads and clear across the River, so close were they to us Darkness and the gunboats determined our persistent foe to fall back and thus at dark we found ourselves crowded like a flock of sheep on the bluffs around the Landing just able to keep the Wolf at bay while the favoring night that settled down on friend and foe put an end to the fearful slaughter for the day a parallel to which this Continent had never before witnessed

Battle of Shiloh or Pittsburgh Landing   Second Day's Battle

April 7th No pen can tell, no hand can paint no words can utter the horrors of last night. Such a doleful pressure of misery and woe and suffering as rested on this field of *death* Unable to succor or help the poor wounded men that fell in yesterdays battle the living cared only for themselves Scarcely able to endure the great fatigue of the day each one cared only for himself

The enemy held undisputed possession of the greater portion of the field where lay the badly wounded About 10 o'clock at night the thick smoke in the air gathered in thunder clouds lit up by flashes of lightning and rolling thunder — and soon the rain began to come down in torrents drenching both man and beast [29] There was no shelter any place Piles of provisions and ammunition lay uncovered. The darkness was impenetrable except when the lightning flashed

The groans of the *wounded* and *dying* could be heard in the din of the tempest The struggles of the wounded horses as they floundered upon the ground and came running through the darkness made the situation one of almost as much danger as during the day in the battle. Signal lights were flashing on the river all night as the boats kept constantly running back and forth bringing Buells Army across which yesterday marched thirty miles to

[29] Grant himself wrote of this night: "During the night rain fell in torrents and our troops were exposed to the storm without shelter. I made my headquarters under a tree a few hundred yards back from the river bank. My ankle was so much swollen from the fall of my horse the Friday night preceding, and the bruise was so painful, that I could get no rest. The drenching rain would have precluded the possibility of sleep without this additional cause. Some time after midnight, growing restive under the storm and the continuous pain, I moved back to the log-house under the bank. This had been taken as a hospital, and all night wounded men were being brought in, their wounds dressed, a leg or an arm amputated as the case might require, and everything being done to save life or alleviate suffering. The sight was more unendurable than encountering the enemy's fire, and I returned to my tree in the rain." Grant, *Personal Memoirs*, 1:349.

be here at the fight which was impending As the poor tired fellows came up from the landing they gave a *shout* and a *cheer* and yelled "Never mind boys We'll *lick hell* out of them to-morrow" Such a welcome shout made us feel new again But [we] thought of the fearful morrow and would it be possible to redeem the terrible losses of to-day.

It took all night to get that army of 30,000 men across the Tennessee Before dawn this mighty Army of reenforcements was in line of battle. Before the darkness had lifted from the deep forest we heard the roll of musketry and the shouts of Buells men far to the front — at first the scattering shots of the pickets then the increasing crash of the small arms followed by the roar of the cannon and the cheers of the contending hosts as they grappled in the death struggle for the old field of yesterday About 10 oclock our scattered Regiment got together about 400 men and we marched out toward the front and took our place in the reserve in line of battle near where we fought on yesterday Here we lay more as a Reserve than anything else

Buells Army to-day is doing the *fighting* The cannonading at this time was *terrific* and on until in the afternoon. Batteries were *taken* and *retaken*. Sometimes one side held the ground then the other would rally and recapture it, and the roll of the musketry from 60,000 guns intermixed with the noise of the cannon and the bursting shells made the earth tremble with the concussion — as the two giants grappled in the final struggle for the victory. This desperate fighting lasted about 4 hours Acres and acres of timber such as small saplings and large underbrush were mowed down and trees one foot in diameter were cut down as if a mowing machine had gone through the field and limbs fell like autumn leaves in the leaden and iron storm. Men and horses were piled in death over hundreds of acres on the fatal field[30]

At last! At last! About 3 oclock there was precipitate haste to the front and the fire seemed to slacken and the volleys of musketry were getting more distant toward the South Soon the glad news came that the enemy was *retreating* No shipwrecked sailors on a desert island famished and ready to die ever hailed a passing vessel with more delight and joy than every one on the Union side hailed that glad news. Men mortaly wounded

[30] For Buell's own account of this day's battle, see Buell, "Shiloh Reviewed," 775–9; *Official Records*, Series I, Vol. X, Part I, 293–5.

jumped upon their feet and shouted for *Victory* Every coward who had slunk under the river bank was out of his hole There had not been so many men *wanting* to go to the front since the battle began The woods were full of Cavalry hunting the *front* They had heard that the enemy was "retreating" and they wanted to give him some of their ammunition

Two or three of us took a little ramble out on the field and we perhaps went one mile or more from the Regt. We took a look at the ghastly sights By this time we had become accustomed to seeing *dead* men and the *shock* had passed We soon came to where the dead lay thick The first dead rebel I came to lay on his back with his hands raised above his head and had died in great agony I took a *button* from his coat Here was the camp of the 52d Ills Federal and Confederate lay alternately scattered over the ground some of them wounded and so near dead from exposure that they were mostly insane

Farther on the dead and wounded became more numerous Some had died in a quiet and peaceful manner and had passed away with no visible sign of pain or suffering Others wore the most fearful signs of agony as they had struggled with death Some fell with their muskets tightly gripped in both hands so that they could scarcely be separated I saw five *dead* Confederates all killed by one six pound solid shot — no doubt from one of our cannon They had been behind a log and all in a row The ball had raked them as they crouched behind the log (no doubt firing at our men) One of them had his *head* taken off One had been struck at the right shoulder and his chest lay open. One had been cut in two at the bowels and nothing held the carcass together but the spine. One had been hit at the thighs and the legs were torn from the body. The fifth and last one was piled up into a mass of skull, arms, some toes and the remains of a butternut suit. Just a few feet from where they lay the cannon ball had struck a large tree and lodged. I took it out and carried it some distance but finaly threw it down as it became too heavy a relic to carry.

I saw one Union man leaning against a tree with a violin tightly grasped in his left hand. He had been dead some time and had no doubt been instantly killed Another close by was leaning against a tree with his hat pulled down over his eyes and his hands crossed in front of him. I thought him asleep but when I took his hat off I found him cold and *dead*. This was in the camp of Genl Prentiss who was on the extreme front and where our men were first surprised yesterday morning I saw where the 3d Iowa and some other regiments fought yesterday there has been the most terrible destruction I counted 26 dead battery horses on a few square rods of ground and the men were lying almost in heaps Blue and gray sleep together[31] Oh my God! Can there be anything in the *future* that *compensates* for this slaughter Only Thou knowest

Around these batteries men have died at their posts beside the guns Some are torn all to pieces leaving nothing but their heads or their boots Pieces of clothing and *strings of flesh* hang on the limbs of the trees around them — and the faithful horses have died *in the harness* right by the cannon. Some of them torn to quarters by the bursting shells and their swollen bodies are already filling the air with a deadly odor.

While here some cavalry came dashing back and yelled that the enemy was coming on us again in force The way we climbed toward the Regiment was not very *slow* But we lost our course and the sky being clouded we could not tell directions The woods were full of men running in all directions and we were in the flood of a *great panic* Some said the River was in one direction and others said it was the *opposite* We crawled into a *thicket* and waited until we got a little better settled in our minds about the *direction* Finaly we got the course and went on until we [saw] some of our Regiment[32]

The enemy has retreated and left all his dead and wounded on the field We have whipped him but at an awful *sacrifice* The two armies are like two tenacious *bull dogs*. They have grappled and fought until both are exhausted and worn out. One has crawled away to *lie down* and the other

[31] Grant visited the battlefield on this day, also. "Shiloh was the severest battle fought at the West during the war, and but few in the East equalled it for hard, determined fighting. I saw an open field, in our possession on the second day, over which the Confederates had made repeated charges the day before, so covered with dead that it would have been possible to walk across the clearing, in any direction, stepping on dead bodies, without a foot touching the ground." Grant, *Personal Memoirs*, 1:355-6.

[32] Lt. S. D. Thompson of the 3rd Iowa reported that this was a ruse to get the soldiers off the field: ". . . whole regiments scattered into squads and scattered over the field in search of their dead and wounded; and it was not long before the entire field was covered with stragglers and plunderers of the dead. To put a stop to this, the Cavalry was ordered to get up a panic among them. They rode frantically over the field, circulating the report that the enemy's cavalry was upon them. The effect was admirable. In a few minutes the panic communicated itself to all parts of the field, and stragglers without number poured through the woods toward the river like a herd of frightened brutes. No one could tell what he was running from. . . ." Thompson, *Recollections with the Third Iowa*, 241.

one *cannot follow*. This is our condition We are quite glad to hold the *ground and let him retreat*

Ambulances and men are hurrying over the field and gathering up the wounded The surgeons are *cutting* off the arms and legs Burying parties and details are out burying the dead this evening who have been dead now since Sunday Morning The air is already filled with the stench of decaying bodies. The battle field is one vast forest with here and there an old field The soil is poor and clayey and some of the ground swampy and some rolling covered with briers and thick underbrush

The terrible rain of last night has filled the ground with water and washed the gullies out The trees are just bursting into leaf and the little flowers are covering the ground — but their fragrance is lost in the pall of death which has settled down on this bloody field

"This is the valley and the shadow of death"

PART II

PITTSBURG LANDING TO IUKA, MISSISSIPPI

April 8, 1862 to September 20, 1862

The Siege of Corinth

Camp at Battlefield of Shiloh

April 8th [1862] Some of us slept in the tents of the 8th Iowa last night. The Tents of the 8th and 12th Iowa are close together and the men are *missing* — nearly all of them were taken prisoners on Sunday[1] Here are the knapsacks and blankets just as left when the fight commenced at daylight on Sunday morning and the men had only time to get their guns and fall in or rather to fall out and go to fighting. They never saw their baggage again.

The rain kept falling all night There was a great *panic* this morning caused by men firing off their guns to see if the *loads* would go out There was a rally on the color line and we expected another fight It is very chilly and thousands of the wounded lay out the *third* night with no care Burial squads have been busy all day burrying the *dead* Our *losses* are thought to be from 15,000 to 20,000 men and the enemies much greater [2] Have been trying to get our Company together but cannot find all the men Granville Feagins was killed and left on the field of Sunday Oscar Ford was mortally wounded and is now dead Lieut Fisk is missing likewise

[1] The 8th Iowa lost 379 men captured, the 12th lost 429 captured, in the Battle of Shiloh. *The War of the Rebellion . . . Official Records . . .*, Series I, Vol. X, Part I, 101. (Hereafter listed as *Official Records*.)

[2] On the first day of battle, April 6, the Union forces numbered some 40,000 men; the Confederate, about 44,000. On Monday, April 7, the Union forces had been raised to about 54,000, while the Confederates had dropped to 34,000. Casualties on the Union side were: 1,754 killed, 8,408 wounded, and 2,885 missing or captured; a total of 13,047. Confederate losses were: 1,728 killed, 8,012 wounded, and 959 captured or missing; a total of 10,699. *Official Records*, Series I, Vol. X, Part I, 108, 391; Joseph W. Rich, *The Battle of Shiloh* (Iowa City, 1911), 89-90. Grant questioned the accuracy of the Confederate figures, claiming that his burial parties estimated a total of 4,000 buried from both armies. *Personal Memoirs of U. S. Grant* (2 vols., New York, 1885), 1:367.

Crosly and some others Some fifteen men of Co "G" are wounded and some of them badly All the wounded are being hurried on hospital boats and will be sent away

Today an advanced column of our army encountered a detachment of the enemy and quite a skirmish took place This afternoon we were assigned to Laumans Brigade [3] and we went out a couple of miles to the South We have lost about all our blankets and knapsacks and have nothing but hard bread to eat which has no more taste or substance than a *shingle* This has been a cold and stormy day and the mud is about knee deep

April 9th Weather damp and rainy Went down to the Landing this forenoon to hunt up some of our baggage which we left on the boat Thousands of men were there getting their teams and camp equipments Wounded and sick men were lying around on the muddy ground and the dead were being tramped over as if they were logs of wood I helped to carry two poor fellows on a boat who had the measles and were too weak to help themselves. They had lain there two days they said The hillside at the Landing is so deep in mud as to be almost impassable

I slipped a few lines into an envelope and gave it to a stranger and asked him to *mail* it somewhere so that it would go to the folks at home and let them know that we are not as bad off as we *might* be All mails are stoped and no letters will be taken from here unless *smuggled* through This has been a *terrible* battle and the news must not go North for a few days until the Reports can be *fixed* up This afternoon I took a stroll out about three miles. I have not eat anything to-day and have been so sickened that I shall not want anything for sometime

Where the retreat commenced on Monday afternoon are hundreds and thousands of wounded rebels They had fallen in heaps and the woods had taken fire and burned all the clothing off them and the naked and blackened corpses are still lying there unburied On the hillside near a deep hollow our men were hauling them down and throwing them into the deep gulley *One hundred and eighty* had been thrown in when I was there. Men were in on top of the *dead* straightening out their legs and arms and *tramping* them down so as to make the hole contain as many as possible Other men on the hillside had ropes with a noose on one end and they would attach

[3] Brig.-Gen. Jacob G. Lauman commanded the Third Brigade of the Fourth Division of the Army of the Tennessee. At Shiloh this Brigade had consisted of the 31st and 44th Indiana and the 17th and 25th Kentucky. *Official Records*, Series I, Vol. X, Part I, 103.

this to a mans foot or his head and haul him down to the hollow and roll him in Where the ground was level it was so full of water that the excavation filled up as fast as dug and the corpse was just rolled in and the earth just thrown over it and left

War is *hell* broke *loose* and benumbs all the tender feelings of men and makes of them *brutes* I do not want to see any more such scenes and yet I would not have missed this for any consideration

April 13th Sunday The three days between these dates has been occupied in getting into shape again and looking after the *dead* and *wounded* General Grant is blamed with this great *disaster* [4] All think that the troops had no discipline here Some of them had been here a week or two and not a single fortification had been made. [5] The pickets were surprised on the morning of the battle and consequently the whole army was *surprised* Our men should have known that the enemy had a strong force at Corinth 25 miles away. . .[6]

[4] The "blame" for Shiloh was long disputed. Certainly, the men who fought there had no love for Grant, but great admiration for Buell. A member of the 2nd Iowa wrote on April 16th: "I have ridden over the whole field, in every division, and am a frequenter at Grant's headquarters, and speak the sentiments of *the army* when I say that Gen. Grant is responsible for much of the terrible sacrifice of life on the 6th." Keokuk *Weekly Gate City*, Apr. 30, 1862. W. H. Clune of the 6th Iowa concluded that "General Buell is unquestionably the hero of Pittsburgh, and from what they say of his management yesterday can go to bed and forget more generalship in one night than Gen. Grant ever knew." *Ibid.*, Apr. 23, 1862.

[5] "The criticism has often been made that the Union troops should have been intrenched at Shiloh. Up to that time the pick and spade had been but little resorted to at the West. I had, however, taken this subject under consideration soon after reassuming command in the field, and . . . my only military engineer reported unfavorably. Besides this, the troops with me, officers and men, needed discipline and drill more than they did experience with the pick, shovel and axe. Reinforcements were arriving almost daily, composed of troops that had been hastily thrown together into companies and regiments—fragments of incomplete organizations, the men and officers strangers to each other. Under all these circumstances I concluded that drill and discipline were worth more to our men than fortifications." Grant, *Personal Memoirs*, 1:357-8.

[6] The officers in command of course knew that the Confederate troops were concentrated at Corinth—having retreated there after the defeat at Fort Donelson in February. When Grant took over the command of the Army of the Tennessee in March he planned to concentrate his forces at Pittsburg Landing and, after Buell's forces had arrived, to move against Corinth. What the officers did not seem to know, on the morning of April 6, was that the Confederate General, A. S. Johnston, had moved his forces out of Corinth toward Pittsburg in great strength on April 3. *Ibid.*, 330–36; William Preston Johnston, "Albert Sidney Johnston and the Shiloh Campaign," *Century Magazine*, 29:621 (February, 1885).

Only 35 men are able for duty[7]   The bad water and the hard fare has given them the diarrhea   Many can not stand from weakness.   Am sick myself and have suffered a great deal for the last two nights

April 14th   Almost all sick and the *blues* prevail in the most malignant form [8]

April 15th   Moved Camp to-day about two miles farther out on the battlefield   We are on the front and the enemies pickets not far away [9] We found a good camping place on a hill side with water and wood convenient. . . . Hard times are upon us and many of the boys wish they were at *home*   Poor fellows I pity them   Some of them are suffering much and we can take but little care of them   Not more than one third of the Company can take care of themselves.   I am not disappointed by these hard times   The war must go on until a successful end is reached no difference what the sacrifice may be. . . .

April 17th   How we wish Dr Fisk was with us now   To night there are rumors of an attack and we sleep on our Arms.

[7] The 15th Iowa had lost a total of 185 men in the two-day battle at Shiloh: 21 killed, 156 wounded, and 8 captured or missing. *Official Records*, Series I, Vol. X, Part I, 105. Of Company G, which probably numbered around 150 at the time of the battle, 1 man was killed, 14 wounded, and 2 captured, one of whom was Lieut. Fisk. *History of the Fifteenth Regiment, Iowa Veteran Volunteer Infantry* . . . (Keokuk, 1887), 558–62, 579.

[8] Lieut. S. D. Thompson, 3rd Iowa, reported: "The sanitary condition of the army was anything but flattering. Of our own regiment which, so far as we could hear, was a type of all the rest, very few were even in tolerable health. Fevers and camp diarrhoea [sic] filled the hospitals to overflowing; the sick lists increased rapidly; and the great extent to which the army was weakened in numbers by sickness, became a just source of alarm. It became painfully evident, too, that its *morale* was being greatly impaired by the same cause. . . . It will not be surprising, then, that many good soldiers were possessed of a *homesickness*—a desire to be sent home on furlough or discharged, that amounted almost to a mania." S. D. Thompson, *Recollections with the Third Iowa Regiment* (Cincinnati, 1864), 258.

[9] General P. G. T. Beauregard withdrew his Confederate forces to Corinth, some twenty miles southwest of Shiloh, following the Union victory on April 7. The Union forces, now under the personal command of Major-General Henry W. Halleck, with Grant second in command, inched slowly toward Corinth during April and May, in spite of the fact that Halleck's forces were vastly superior to those of Beauregard. A reporter on the scene, Albert D. Richardson, wrote: "Halleck's line was ten miles in length. The grand army was like a huge serpent, with its head pinned on our left, and its tail sweeping slowly around toward Corinth. Its majestic march was so slow that the Rebels had ample warning. It was large enough to eat up Beauregard at one mouthful; but Halleck crept forward at the rate of about three-quarters of a mile per day. Thousands and thousands of his men died from fevers and diarrhea." Otto Eisenschiml and Ralph Newman, *The American Iliad: The Epic Story of the Civil War* . . . (Indianapolis 1947), 276.

April 18th Have had a hard time of it until about 4 o'clock since which I feel better. It was so hot that I went out in the shade and lay all day upon the ground There is scarcely a well man in the Company The climate, water and food has about finished us up There was an Inspection of Arms this eve but I was not able to clean my gun No Newspapers are allowed in camp and we do not know what is going on We are said to be about 15 miles from Corinth — a strongly fortified place where the enemy is making a stand and preparing to give us battle. . .

April 21st Weather cool and chilly Has rained for five days and the roads are impassable This is the most Godforsaken country I ever saw We move camp about every day and in the woods all the time This is one vast *graveyard* and shall we never get out of it The rains have washed the earth from the dead men and horses *Skulls* and *toes* are sticking from beneath the clay all around and the heavy wagons *crush* the bodies turning up the bones of the burried, making this one vast *Golgotha* Sometimes our tents come over a little mound where sleep some unknown soldier who has *died* for a principle but his *servivors* [sic] have not even marked his last resting place or given him the burrial of a *faithful dog* What a mockery these lines seem —

"Blest are the brave who sink to rest
With all their Country's wishes blest"

April 24th This blank between dates was caused by my illness not having been able to write This afternoon cannon could be heard in the direction of Corinth There is constant skirmishing on the picket lines between the two armies. We shall have plenty to do within a few days We have been much better to-day and hope to be ready for duty to-morrow We can scarcely get men enough for guard duty and the few who are able have to be on about all the time Much dissatisfaction exists in the Regiment in regard to some of our field officers Some of whom are notoriously incompetent The Col does not know the difference between file right and file left and is as ignorant of Military Maneuvers as a child[10]

April 25th This has been a cold and dismal day Late this afternoon we

[10] The Colonel of the 15th, Hugh T. Reid, in spite of the fact that he was a "citizen soldier" like the rest of his regiment, was a capable officer. In 1863 he was promoted to the rank of brigadier-general, on the recommendation of General Grant, who did not give his promotions lightly. A. A. Stuart, *Iowa Colonels and Regiments . . .* (Des Moines, 1865), 286. Boyd here displays an attitude typical of the soldiers of the Union army, who were constantly and often unduly critical of those in command.

received orders to move to the westward We took down our tents in the rain Sick men were compelled to get out and get along the best they could. Every man who could stand up had to come into the ranks The roads were awful and the mule drivers swore without ceasing Went two miles and pitched our tents in the swamp We had to cut brush to lay over the water before we could lay our blankets down to make a bed and thus we will try to sleep. On almost every side there are tents stretching away in a continuous line of battle which is many miles in length Lieut Hanks is very sick and looks dreadful bad Cunningham goes around and looks out chances to put all the work on the orderly sergt that he can

April 26th. . . To-day we were put into a Brigade with the 11th 13th and 16th Iowa under acting Brigadier General M. M. Crocker [11] . . .

April 27th Sunday. . . The Chaplain preached to-day in camp He gave a short and appropriate address and it was listened to with much attention He counseled the men to abstain as much as possible from Sabbath breaking and profane language I also heard *Cousin* John Steele of the 13th Ills [Iowa] preach He is an earnest good man. News came this evening that the enemy is advancing There was a great stir in camp and a close examination of guns and ammunition The enemy is not far off and we may expect a bloody battle at any time

Have been drilling about all day Lieut Col Dewey does about all the Regimental drilling Under the *inspiration* of about a quart of old Commissary he can worry us out in two hours Some of the men are sick and are so badly discouraged that nothing but the presence of death will make them move at all A great battle has seemed imminent for the last two weeks and on this account many men have been *very weak* On Dress Parade this eve news was read that New Orleans has been captured [12] This cheered the men much and they did make the woods ring and the cheer was taken up by other regiments and Brigades and it could be heard for miles as it rolled along the extended front

[11] This is the famous "Crocker's Iowa Brigade." It was the Third Brigade, Sixth Division, Army of the Tennessee. Brigadier-General Marcellus M. Crocker, of Des Moines, had studied for two years at West Point, but resigned because of ill health. He studied law at Fairfield; in 1855 he moved to Des Moines. He had entered the Union Army as a captain in Company D, 2nd Iowa, but was almost at once elected major of the Regiment. In October, 1861, he became colonel of the 13th Iowa. His Iowa Brigade became one of the most distinguished in the Army of the Tennessee. *Ibid.*, 255–64.

[12] New Orleans fell to Admiral Farragut on April 25, 1862.

Advance on Corinth

April 29th The roar of cannon has been heard for about two hours to the Southwest. About half past 11 o'clock we were hurried into line of battle by Col Dewey Were ordered to prepare one days rations and be ready *within* fifteen minutes to march At the call of the drum we came into line With the balance of the Brigade and under the command of General Crocker we marched in a westerly direction Did not permanently halt until about 9 o'clock at night, having marched about nine miles through a heavy forest The air was very chilly and we were not allowed to build any fires We tried to sleep on the cold damp ground Saw a few cabins in the woods as we came along Met some Cavalry who told us that they had been out to Purdy and burned a railroad Bridge [13]

April 30th At break of day we were called into line and given ten minutes to eat a "hard tack" and a little raw meat and then we went onward for about one mile and a half when we halted We about faced and at 11 oclock we were back in camp Have orders to keep one days rations in our haversacks

May 1st This morning at 7 A M we struck tents and with the whole Brigade started Southwest to some unknown destination Travelled slowly until 1 PM and in line of battle stacked arms. At sundown the wagons came up with our tents and camp equipage and we were soon keeping house This is the best camping ground we have yet seen so I think we will not stay long Wood and water are handy Came six miles to day and we are now supposed to be off the old battle field of Shiloh. . .

May 2d We are now ten miles from [Pittsburg] Landing Weather fine and warm This afternoon did some washing for myself There are thousands of troops ahead of us and we shall soon go forward again

May 3rd Moved again to-day in a southwesterly direction with one days cooked rations At 4 oclock we again pitched our tents in a wheat field The wheat is heading out — but this is about as far as this wheat will *advance* This days travel extended about seven or eight miles The country has been rolling and mostly heavy timber This evening for about one hour there was heavy cannonading south of here Some of our troops are feeling [out] the enemies position

[13] This was probably a bridge on the Mobile & Ohio R. R., which passed a few miles west of Purdy and ran through Corinth. Purdy, Tennessee, lies some twelve miles west and slightly north of Pittsburg Landing.

We are very tired and hungry but just here orderlies call beat and I had to go to Head-quarters and here Col Dewey ordered us to see that 4 days rations were cooked and to be ready to *march* The men cooked until 10 o'clock and we filled our haversacks I hope our Army will not attack the enemy to-morrow as it is Sunday and our men seem to have a dread of going into battle on that day unless in *defence* The terrible Sunday at Pittsburgh is pointed to and the reason given that the enemy was defeated because they commenced the fight on that day A great battle seems near at hand and the *fate* of one of these armies will be decided here to all appearances We have about 120,000 men here and the enemy is supposed to have about the same number We advance with no possible retreat and against strong fortifications We are going ahead with all possible assurance Genl Halleck Gen Grant and Genl Buell are all here with us[14] Genl Grant is hated and *despised* by all the men and cursed ever since the 6th of April. . .

May 5th. . . Are hourly expecting to march toward Corinth and have cooked ahead two or three days rations. . .

May 6th We drilled four hours to-day Major Belknap came in this evening and told us to cook 4 days rations and be prepared to march at 10 o'clock to morrow morning

May 7th We marched at the time named Came 2 miles and halted 2 hours in the hot sun until the Brigade could be assigned a place Our place came in a big patch of brush and we went to grubbing. E. P. Bye and I made a bed of round poles Saw the 3d Iowa and they are camped near us.[15] The same rolling land and heavy timber continues The farms we saw are almost all deserted and the fences burned up In front of our Camp is a heavy fortification and is designed to keep our *relatives* within from coming out too hastily No one seems to know much about this coun-

[14] Halleck, who took command of the army after Shiloh, had three armies under him: the Army of the Ohio, commanded by Don Carlos Buell; the Army of the Mississippi, commanded by John Pope; and the Army of the Tennessee, commanded by George H. Thomas. Grant was second in command of the whole. Thomas' army, to which Crocker's Iowa Brigade was attached, was on the right; Buell was in the center; and Pope on the left wing of the advance on Corinth. The three armies numbered about 120,000 men; Beauregard at Corinth had an estimated strength of about 70,000. Grant, *Personal Memoirs*, 1:371-2, 376.

[15] For the experiences of the 3rd and other Iowa regiments in this advance, see Thompson, *Recollections with the Third Iowa,* Henry H. Wright, *A History of the Sixth Iowa Infantry* (Iowa City, 1923); Olynthus B. Clark (ed.), *Downing's Civil War Diary* [11th Iowa] (Des Moines, 1916).

try nor what the enemy is doing The siege of Corinth will now commence and we may now say this is the "First Epistle to the Corinthians". . .

May 9th. . . Heavy cannonading has been going on all day in a southeasterly direction[16]

May 10th No wind stirring and the day has been hot. Were notified this forenoon to be ready with one days rations in haversacks and to be ready to march at a moments warning Just at 12 o'clock we were ordered into line and started southeast. Marched until about 5 o'clock and halted Co "G" was ordered to report at Hd quarters for "Picket" duty Major Belknap acted as *guide* and went with us out one mile and a half where we went on duty — putting out 27 men and keeping 12 men for a Reserve

May 11th Nothing in the shape of an enemy disturbed us last night, and nothing alarmed us more than the shadow of some bush or the dark form of an old stump The owls *hooted* around in the trees and made it seem lonely But we prefer owls or any other birds to *secesh* About 12 o'clock at night I being a sergt of the guard went around to relieve the pickets and as I was going through some thick brush and not counting correctly I had got one post too far and came upon a green Dutchman belonging to another command As a streak of moonlight came through the trees and a little rustling of the bushes revealed me to him he yelled H-a-l-t The Dutchman was behind a tree with his bayonet fixed I of course *halted* when he said who comes *dere* I answered "Friend with the countersign" Said he *advance* and give the countersign As soon as I advanced he cocked his musket and took *aim* at me and yelled "Corporal of the guard" and at the same time told me not to move and *I did not move* When the Corporal came I went forward and gave him the countersign (which was Lexington) and it was all right Were not relieved until 8 o'clock I shall never forget this our first night on "Picket" nor the excited Dutchman

May 12th Weather very hot Our camp is on the southern slope of a hill News came to-day that Memphis has been taken and also Island No. 10. Also Norfolk Va[17] and another rumor says the enemy is about to

---

[16] Skirmishes between opposing picket lines took place almost constantly during this advance. This incident probably was that around Farmington, Mississippi. *Official Records*, Series I, Vol. X, Part I, 729.

[17] This illustrates the age-old unreliability of camp gossip. Island No. 10 had been captured by Union forces on April 7; while Memphis, Tennessee, did not fall until June 6. Norfolk, Virginia, had been captured on May 9, and the news could have reached the troops before Corinth by this time.

evacuate Corinth Lieut Col Dewey called all the Orderlies up to his tent this eve and gave us a grand old *Cussing* because we do not get more men out to drill He swore if we did not do better he would have us all reduced to the *ranks*. (I do not care a red if he does) He also went around the officers tents and gave them a blessing according to the strength of the Commissary he had aboard

May 13th This morning we received orders to be ready to move — but were ordered out to drill awhile and kept at it until 10 o'clock when we were recalled and got into line and at 12 oclock marched out on the main road leading to Corinth and went straight forward for two miles and camped in the thick timber on the right of the road Have lots of grubbing to do to make a camping place and a drill ground Are said to be within 4 miles of the "Corinthians"

Weather still hot. Hanks being away Capt C[unningham] wants me to sleep in his tent with him He seems to be very *homesick* and tells me he thinks if the *diarrhea* that is now on him lasts a few weeks more he will not be *alive* Weather very hot and an *insect* called *"gray back"* is visiting quite numerously in our camp and has nearly got possession of some of the men

May 14th We were given today to wash our clothes and clean up Col Reid took command in place of Lieut Col Dewey This evening heavy cannonadding was heard to the west[18] Probably our men shelling the woods to find out the whereabouts of the enemy. Water is scarce and we have to dig wells here.

May 15th Weather sultry This morning we got orders to have two days rations in our haversacks and to be prepared to *march* At 11 oclock we were called into line and with the whole Brigade went south quarter of a mile on the Northern side of an open field where our batteries were *masked* We remained here until 2 o'clock when we came back to camp A large force went toward Corinth and we were ordered out as a reserve — A rumor says Corinth has been evacuated Only 33 of our Company were out to-day. Some of the balance were sick and some had the cannon fever...

May 17th Last night there was a great deal of picket firing in front and on the right or west of us. Lay on our arms all night in line of battle. Were

[18] Raids on the two railroads which crossed at Corinth, the Mobile & Ohio and the Memphis & Charleston, took place on May 14. *Official Records*, Series I, Vol. X, Part I, 660.

relieved at 10 o'clock and pulled up stakes and went two miles southeast
Our pickets and scouts drove the enemy's outposts all the way firing over
every foot of ground Saw *six dead men* of the enemies who were killed as
we advanced We had several wounded — We are to-night camped in a
dense heavy wood and very close to the Rebs. Some of the officers look a
good deal *worried* this evening The artillerymen are throwing up breastworks until late tonight

Only 34 of our Company able to march to-day Have had nothing to eat
all day but a hard tack and a piece of raw meat roasted on a stick — Heavy
artillery firing all day toward the west The muskets have been cracking
close ahead of us all day Weather hot and dry.

Siege of Corinth

May 18th Sunday There was a great deal of picket firing all last night
Detailed 10 men to build breastworks Thousands of men are felling tim-
bers and digging like beavers Went over to the 13th and saw Cousin John
Steele. While there several rebel cannon balls came over from the "Corinthians" Heavy works are building around the entire line which must be
about 12 miles They are about four feet high made of solid timber in
front (or on our side) and ties about ten feet long run out The base is
about 10 feet wide and at the top four feet thick Openings for cannon are
made at intervals The ditch is dug out on our side of the work which
gives the men better protection This eve we are ordered to have 2 days
rations in our haversacks A rumor is out that we will assault the enemies
works to-morrow and the consequence is that the *sick* list is largely *increased* If this should prove *true* that we make a *raid* tomorrow I have got
a good big *Corn cake* and a bottle of *molasses* and *three* potatoes which I
shall carry with me into the disturbance

Capt Cunningham is getting quite *feeble* at the same time quite *confidential* He says he is either going *home* or he is going to make some
money He says there will be some fine chances to steal cotton after awhile
and that if any chance comes close to him it shall not pass He says it
don't make any *difference* how a man *makes* his money just so he has plenty
of it (I think it does and if this is the *key* to this mans soul he will bear
watching)

Capt Cunningham says he wants me to tell the men who lounge around
his tent and pick off *gray backs* on a hot day that it is very *disagreeable* to
him and must be *stoped* Oh yes said I *certainly* Guess when I go and

tell those poor emaciated sick boys (some of whom are not many days travel from their graves) why I will set up all night and catch *gray backs* and put them in a pin-box and empty them under the fly of his tent *that's all* If he had one half the courage of a healthy *gray back* he would tell them himself

May 19th Received orders to march at 10 o'clock At that time we had tents struck and knapsacks all packed Just then word came that the Rebs were advancing upon us, and we were again ordered *not to move* Only 25 effective men could be got into line The mumps are raging in the Army and every other disease known to human beings I have the jaundice and am as yellow as a Yankee pumpkin and so billious I cannot keep anything down that I eat and oh how sick I am (especially when I hear the *pickets* firing) All the officers trunks and valuables were taken to the rear to-day and this eve they were brought back again It looks like it was even *dangerous* to be *safe*. Heavy firing all around and we can hear our shells burst over in the enemies lines

May 20th Hard rain last night and to-day is cloudy Heavy artillery fire all day but mostly on our left in Shermans Division or Corps. The rebs throw shells into Shermans camps. . . The cars seem to be busy over in Corinth. We can hear them whistle and running day and night [19] Genl Mitchell joined Genl Pope on the east to-day with 20,000 more men and more reinforcements are coming to help *bag* this batch of Rebs All able bodied men are at work on the entrenchments

May 21st This has been a very exciting day in camp At 10 oclock the Union Brigade moved over on our right over one mile in advance of the line of entrenchments in order to erect new works The enemies outposts resisted this most savagely and with three or four Regiments of Infantry hurried up gave our men a warm time Our side brought up a few pieces of art[illery] and held their ground Orders again to have two days rations in our haversacks A continuous crash of musketry continued all day at the front which sounded like a general engagement A number of men have been killed on both sides to-day Several Commissioned officers

[19] "Trains of cars were heard coming in and going out of Corinth constantly. Some of the men who had been engaged in various capacities on the railroads before the war claimed that they could tell, by putting their ears to the rail, not only which way the trains were moving but which trains were loaded and which were empty. They said loaded trains had been going out for several days and empty ones coming in. Subsequent events proved the correctness of their judgment." Grant, *Personal Memoirs*, 1:380.

of our Regiment have *resigned* of late and gone home   Capt [Wilson T.] Smith Co "B" Lieut [Charles M. I.] Reynolds Co "D" and Lieut [Ebenezer E.] Herbert Co "C" have disappeared   A good many straight guesses are made as to why men *resign* about such a time as this   Those who cannot resign will of course have to remain   I hear of no men who carry a *musket* resigning.

May 22d   Weather warm and a great amount of shooting on the picket line last night and at day break a heavy skirmish occured in front of our camp   Col Reid was around among the tents at 4 oclock telling the men (in a *whisper*) that we were expecting an attack and to be up and into line

May 23d   Weather cloudy and wet   Have been unwell all day   I can't eat — have the jaundice too bad.   Shuler of "K" ran away from the Hospital at Monterey back ten miles — and came running into camp crazy as a *bed bug*   He had torn most of his clothing off and all bruised and a horrible sight.   16 men was all we could get out to drill to-day

May 24th   Rained all last night   Have been helping to fix up some bunks for the sick boys   Charley Nicholls is very sick and I think a few more days will take him *from here*   All the men look bad   Their energy and ambition has almost left them   All of them have the diarrhea and are scarcely able to take care of themselves   The *dead march* can be heard at all times from sun up until sun down in the camps around us — as they take one, two or three poor fellows and lay them in this cold and dismal wilderness in graves to be forever unknown   Not even a coffin is provided   Lumber cannot be had.   Shuler who came in crazy yesterday died to-day   If we remain here until July but few will be *alive*   Some of the men joke and laugh while they are laying out the dead and seem to think nothing of it   How inhuman and wicked this thing called War   It brutalizes men and crushes out all Christian feeling

May 25th Sunday   A fine day.   Had Reg Inspection at 10 o'clock and I had a time getting the poor sick fellows out — or enough of sick and well to make any kind of a showing for a Company   After inspection the Chaplain preached   Have had some rest today   If the people at home knew how the sick soldiers are treated in this Army there would be such a howl of indignation and cursing as would make the country *tremble*   There is said to be 25,000 sick men in this Army   The officers nearly all want to go *home* but had rather see their men burried than let them leave if they knew they would get well by going away a few weeks. . . .

Three of our company died yesterday — Jeffries the *semi* colored man and little Lewis Skank and Charles Nicholls The two latter had the typhoid fever and Jeffries had an arm amputated since the battle of Shiloh. I ate a lot of *desicated* (should be desecrated) vegetables yesterday and they have made me the sickest of my life I shall never want any more such fodder Serg't Dan Embree has the mumps and he lies on his back in a little wedge tent standing in the sun He is "Commissary" for the Company and the hard tack and *sow-belly* are all around him. The heat is about 120 deg inside the tent and the grease is running away and leaving nothing but the skin of the hog, the hard tack and Dan I think this is a good time *not* to have the mumps. . .

Evacuation of Corinth

May 30*th* A series of heavy explosions occured about 5 o'clock this morning to the southwest which evidenty were not cannon 10 o'clock news just came that the enemy has crawled out of Corinth and left us *holding the bag* The explosion this morning was caused by the enemy blowing up some buildings and magazines which they would not *take* with them Some of our men are said to be in Corinth now

Later Several of our regiments have just come from Corinth and say the town is *deserted* and almost everything destroyed Our Cavalry have gone in pursuit southward Some say they are glad they did not stay to make any more *disturbance* and some say they are sorry they have gone These latter fellows are probably *lying* For one I am glad they are gone and they have my permission to keep agoing Hardly a soldier in the whole Army but knew more than one week ago that they were going to *retreat* because we could hear the cars running day & night [20]

[20] Halleck's dilatory operations before Corinth had been, in Grant's opinion, wrong; but Halleck overrode any objections from his subordinate, whom he disliked. The evacuation of Corinth came, to many of the officers, as an anti-climax. Grant wrote: "The possession of Corinth by the National troops was of strategic importance, but the victory was barren in every other particular. It was nearly bloodless. It is a question whether the *morale* of the Confederate troops engaged at Corinth was not improved by the immunity with which they were permitted to remove all public property and then withdraw themselves. On our side I know officers and men of the Army of the Tennessee—and I presume the same is true of those of the other commands—were disappointed at the result. They could not see how the mere occupation of places was to close the war while large and effective rebel armies existed. They believed that a well-directed attack would at least have partially destroyed the army defending Corinth. For myself I am satisfied that Corinth could have been captured in a two days' campaign commenced promptly on the arrival of reinforcements after the battle of Shiloh." Grant, *Personal Memoirs*, 1:381.

May 31st Have had a half day to clean up and wash   There has been heavy cannonading all day to the South and it is becoming more distant Genl Pope is in hot pursuit of the flying foe. . . .[21]

June 4th Received pay to-day for 4 months Jany 1st to May 1st My own was $80.00   Most of the privates were paid in $50.00 bills (greenbacks) . . .

June 6th. . . When we got back to camp [from a trip to Hamburg] we found tents gone and the regiment had gone away   We followed on after and went through Corinth which has been a good sized town   Has a brick Court House and a few good business houses   One large Hotel called the "Tishomingo House"   Ruin and destruction mark the place   The Rebel Army took everything for use and when they left destroyed all they could Our men are repairing the Railroads   After leaving Corinth we came out one mile and one half southwest and here we found the Regt. . . .

June 10th. . . Major Belknap has command of the Regiment — all the men like him and he knows more about tactics and drilling than all the bal[ance] of the field officers will ever know in their lives. . .

June 15th Sunday We had Regimental Inspection at 9 o'clock after which the men scattered off in all directions   Have been in camp all day Among the 16th Iowa in camp near us there are a great many sick men and many dying Col Chambers Regt   They find one or two dead every morning sometimes in their beds and other times out in the woods   The men are mostly Germans and are a dirty set

June 16th Went on Picket this morning out about one mile and one half We were strung out on a pleasant ridge in the woods   About noon three *cows* came along and we put them in a pen and the boys milked them every *ten minutes* by the "watch"   It is a nice thing to have a little fresh milk in the family   Saw a few prisoners come in also a citizen who said he was tired of war and hoped it would soon end. . .

June 23d Some of the boys went out into the woods this morning and got some fresh meat which they call "Venison" but almost any one else would call it pork   An overseer living close was in camp this morning looking for 19 Negroes that had run away and said he could not hear from them I guess he will not hear from them until *Gabriel calls* This morning Tie Shepherd and I went to a house and asked a young lady at the door

[21] Both Pope and Buell went in pursuit of the Confederates under Beauregard, but abandoned the task after about 30 miles, and returned to Corinth. *Ibid.*, 1:382.

if she would sell us some milk She said she would and filled our canteens
We paid her 25 cents apiece and came back to camp When we examined
the milk we found it *sour* and had to throw it away Besides it spoiled
our canteens But such are the *Secesh*

Camp East of Corinth

July 2d Between these dates we have been following the same old rou-
tine with nothing new to record. We have drilled and drilled in the hot
sun and finaly moved our camp to the suburbs on the East side of Corinth
We are situated in the open woods where there is but little shade yet the
timber has been cleared out and the air can circulate. The ground has been
an old rebel camp and the rubbish and filth that usually accumulates is all
here and more too including several millions of *fleas* and active gray backs
that were not so much afraid of us as their owners were Thousands of
feet of good lumber lay scattered all over the ground and which we have
fallen heir to. The 15th Regt is detailed as Provost Guard and we have
been on duty a few days General Hallecks headquarters are in town Two
Divisions are left here to guard and hold the place They are the 2d and
the 6th Div of the Army of the Tennessee

Sargt Dan Embree and I went down the Railroad and gathered a fine
lot of blackberries which by the way are curing myself and others I almost
live on them and can eat a *peck* at a meal

July 3d Weather hot and sultry Last night there was a grand *row*
close to camp between some soldiers at a house of "ill fame" About one
dozen shots were fired which thoroughly aroused the camp and all sprang
into their clothes and grabbed their guns . . .

July 4th Glorious day. Hot clear and dusty Got a Pass about 9 A M
and went down town The streets were full of soldiers and teams The
Sutlers (the greatest curse of the Army) did well They sold a great quantity of goods and made a lot of money They are the buzzards that follow
the Army Took dinner at the Tishomingo Hotel kept by Herman Wells
formerly of Indianola The best thing we had was *ice* water In the
evening I received two letters and a package of the Indianola "Visitor"
from home. Various rumors are in camp about a battle fought by McClellan
near Richmond Va [22] These rumors have a tremendous effect upon men

[22] This was probably news of one of the many defeats of the inept General George
B. McClellan in the Peninsular Campaign. For a description of this campaign, see
Kenneth P. Williams, *Lincoln Finds a General* (2 vols., New York, 1949), 1:214–41.

as we gain or lose at distance points *So* goes the thermometer of our hopes
and fears in other places

July 5th Have been sick all day Too much Tishomingo ice water &c

July 6th Sunday Bad news from McClellan Army Report says he lost
30,000 men and has fallen back fifteen miles Rebel loss 20,000 men The
Rebels around here are jubilant and say that Beauregard will be back in
a few days and drive us out of these pleasant camping grounds and that
he is already close with a large army These people are either deceived
or else Beauregard is a *fool* We have *settled* here to remain Went to see
a large mineral spring two miles from here South It is sulphurous and
comes up into a large stone basin

The Chaplain is not here now and we have no preaching and Sunday
goes like every other day Men are playing cards all through camp —
selling beer, cooking pies to sell &c This evening I went over North to
see the Rebel grave yard where lie buried 2500 Confederate soldiers the
most of whom perished from wounds received·at Shiloh — and from sickness They have been buried in trenches and laid one above another and
some places are *seven deep* The trenches were continued from day to day
as the mortality called for Here no marble marks the last resting place of
our foes — A paling at the head and a hoop pole tells where lie the *dead*
How sad to look on this scene These silent foes no longer face our flag
The memory of their hate lies buried with them We can but feel that
they were mistaken and deceived and deplore the fate that overtook them
Very few officers are buried here The most of the graves are newly made
and a large majority are marked Louisiana troops

July 7th There is a universal *depression* in camp at the bad news from
Virginia. McClellan is no doubt defeated with immense losses Lieut Hanks
is back with us. Lieut Fisk is a prisoner His folks at home have heard
from him at Montgomery Ala We have 61 men present, 46 for duty 15
absent sick 10 absent with leave and one on detached service My health
and appetite are very treacherous Many of the citizens around here are
coming in with produce They ask 10c per lb for meat. (We can get it
cheaper than that) . . .

July 9th Went out hunting blackberries and found any quantity of
them — filled my bucket and hat and came to camp bareheaded in the
hot sun Great *drunk* in camp Old Sergt Gray had it bad Genl "Beauregard" of Co "K" was on a tremendous spree Rumor says Genl Bragg is

coming against us [23]   News from Va is suppressed and we can learn nothing more. . .

July 15th   The men are beginning to feel too well and some of them stay up about all night to play tricks on one another   The favorite sport is to find some fellow lying asleep and pitch a bucket of water on him — then run and hide in his tent where he is snoring away in a quarter of a minute after he has thrown the water   In these nocturnal sports the innocent often suffer with the guilty

July 16th. . .   Corinth is full of "fast womin" who have come in within a few days and are demoralizing many of the men and with the help of bad whiskey will lay many of them out. The buildings in town are all rented to sutlers merchants and saloon men which bring in a good sum of rent which goes into the Provost "Fund" and is used by the Marshal for the benefit of the Army   Major Belknap has been Marshal but is sick now   Any man found in town without a Pass goes to the guard house. . .   The Regt is decreasing in numbers of about 8 or 9 per day by discharge and desertion   Officers wages have been reduced by Congress of late and Capt C says he does not like it much. . .

July 17th. . .   Embree, McVey and Shepherd and myself made a little foraging trip after the twilight hours   We found *three fowls* high upon an apple tree near the house of a *Native*   We took them under our wings and brought them along to camp   If it had not been for the *dog* we might have got a few more   McClellan rests with his Army on the "James" river 17 miles from Richmond Va

July 19th   Saw Quarter Master Geo W Clark of the 3d Iowa on his way home   He has resigned. He was stoping at the Tishomingo House   Great excitement prevails all over the North. 300,000 more are called for by "old Abe" and volunteering goes on briskly   This is no 90 days war. . .

July 23d   Have been very busy all day with Company business. I have the *blues* and am sick of the way things are managed around the Post   The Officers seem to run everything to make *money* for themselves   Things seem to be getting rather loose. . .

July 27th   We have orders to be ready to march with two days Rations in haversacks and three days in wagons   The whole camp is noisy with preparation   The camp fires to-night look brilliant over the hills as the

---

[23] General Braxton Bragg had replaced Beauregard in command of the Confederate troops in the West.

men are cooking their provisions   Rumor says we will go to Bolivar 45 miles Northwest   Reveille will be at 2 A.M

March to Bolivar Tennessee [24]

July 28th   At 4 o'clock A M we marched   The other three Regiments of the Brigade are along   Went four miles North and passed the last of the field fortifications.   We had a guide who was a Citizen and from some suspicious circumstance he was put under *arrest* and sent back   Before noon about one half the men had thrown away their Knapsacks and Clothing (Extra) and the whole line of March was lined with cast off equipment and clothing   Tall hats with the bird of our country reposing thereon lay strewed in every direction   The sun shone desperately hot and water was scarce and the officers on *horse-back* kept leading on   Crossed the Memphis & Charleston RR at a little town in the woods called Chewalla where some Missouri troops were stationed   Camped at night   Ate a few roasting ears and lay down tired

July 29th   Reveille beat at 3 A.M   My feet hurt me so badly that I could scarcely get up   We found all the Peaches, apples and green corn we wanted   Built a Bridge over the Tuscumbia River and crossed thereon   Heavy timber and hills surround it   The timber is Oak Chestnut and Pine. . .

July 30th   Had a little shower of rain last night   The country traveled over to-day has been quite good and well cultivated   At noon we had a heavy rain which wet us *through*   Camp to-night close to a field of good roasting ears.   There is no *price* set on this Corn as the owner is *absent*   The men have cleaned up all the poultry yards for about two miles each side the line of march   Saw men carrying their boots by the straps while two or three chickens heads would be sticking out.

July 31st   Hundreds of Negroes flock after us and don't seem to be afraid of the soldiers   They yelled and shouted and said "day was glad to see Uncle Sams boys"   With all their ignorance they seem to have pretty good ideas as to what is going on and I think it will not be many months until their influence will be felt in the scale

About 10 oclock we came to Bolivar a beautiful town and surrounded by

[24] This march to Bolivar was to relieve a Union force there under attack. Grant was now in command at Corinth; Halleck had been given command of all the armies on July 11, and had left for Washington. Grant, *Personal Memoirs*, 1:392-3, 396; Williams, *Lincoln Finds a General*, 1:251. Bolivar, Tennessee, is north and west of Corinth, on the Hatchie River.

a splendid country My feet were worn out when we halted and we were all very tired upon this our realy first march Dan and I put up our little tent and will sleep in it to-night I think our tramp has been useless as there is no enemy here in arms

Camp at Bolivar Tennessee

Aug 1st We have a fine camping ground with good spring water handy and are located in fine shady woods. Have been busy all day cleaning off the grounds. The Hatchie River a fine large stream runs close to our camp About 4000 soldiers were in bathing this eve

Aug 2d Sergt Dan Embree, Amos H. Gray and myself are in a mess together Gray is an old Mexican soldier and a graduate in the foraging business What he dont know will not be found out by the bal of us for a long time To-day we went out about two miles and found about 8 acres of a Peach orchard The fruit is the finest I ever saw and the trees were loaded down with fruit We filled our haversacks and came to camp

In the afternoon nearly all of Co "G" went out and we were loaded to the guards with Peaches and on our way home through the thick woods when a squad of armed Pickets took us prisoners and marched us to the headquarters of the officer of the Day who happened to be a Capt in a Ohio Regt. We were kept under guard until almost sundown, when by some desperately hard pleading the Capt let us go to Camp The trouble was our getting outside the picket line There was no picket line when we went out but was thrown out after we left camp We also run a great risk from the rebel cavalry which infest this part of the Country

March to Toombs [Toone's] Station Tennessee

Aug 3d Sunday This forenoon passed off quietly but at noon Lieut Hanks notified us that our Company was ordered to march with two days rations I hurried the men up and soon had them in line Company "E" went along and we were under the Command of Major [William] Purcell of the 16th Ia The day was the hottest of the year but we marched a distance of 8 miles in a northerly direction which brought us to Toombs sta on the Jackson railroad We will sleep in the new Depot to-night. I did not like to march to-day because it was Sunday. . .

Aug 4th Company "E" found a dressed sheep somewhere this morning Major Purcell gave them a healthy old lecture and told the men they would not be allowed to *kill sheep* even if they were away from *home* and that hereafter such men would be severely *punished* Notwithstanding all this

I noticed several pieces of fresh meat coming into camp about noon, and strange as it may appear there was not a hungry man in camp that day

Aug 5th Weather very hot. Several of us went to a house and had a good dinner of Peach Cobbler, New Potatoes &c We enjoyed the meal and no mistake They charged us only 25 cts apiece which was cheap enough

Aug 6th This morning we went out and found plenty of Peaches. Dan and I found a sweet potatoe patch — when we had fairly got down to work digging potatoes a man came out of a house near by with a *gun* at sight of which we silently crept away and *forgot* to leave what potatoes we had dug At 3 o'clock a train (freight) came down from Jackson and we got aboard and came down to Bolivar and into camp A man *died* in Co "E" this eve who was walking around an hour before.

Camp Bolivar Tennessee

Aug 7th Bat drill at 5 oclock this AM and Co drill at 4 P M. I could not attend the latter as I had my clothes in the *suds* The mess business was to-day broken up and the whole Co was consolidated and men detailed to cook I do not like the arrangement Levi Kerr and the two Essex boys are to do the cooking for the Company. . .

Aug 9th Some of the men went out foraging with an escort to-day They brought in a lot of Peaches &c We are living on the substance of the enemy now.[25]

Aug 10th Sunday Had Regimental Inspection at 10 oclock This afternoon I attended a Negro Meeting — About twenty old Negroes run the Noisy part of it and two or three hundred lazy darkeys lay around in the sun and listened Some of them were playing cards and some *marbles* and others were asleep They were dressed in all colors and styles of clothing but most of them were very ragged. . .

Aug 11th Weather hot and I have remained in camp all day or until this evening when Howard Cunningham Dave Myers and I slipped out of camp — dodged up a hollow between two picket posts and went into the country about 2½ miles to inspect a peach orchard and one or two *barn yards*, and finaly came back loaded and crawled back through the picket line and into Camp. . .

Aug 13th A large foraging party was detailed to-day to go out and

[25] "On the 2d of August I was ordered from Washington to live upon the country, on the resources of citizens hostile to the government, so far as practicable." Grant, *Personal Memoirs*, 1:397.

bring in what it would find   A strong guard went along   The party returned with several wagon loads of stuff

Aug 14th   This has been the hottest day I have seen in the South   Half a dozen of our Company went out foraging and brought in two barrels of peaches, a lot of green corn, chickens, Butter &c   Wrote a letter for Indianola Visitor

Aug 15th   Lieut Col Dewey has been appointed Colonel of the 23d Iowa Infty   When this news came the men all through the Regt *cheered* and the cheer finaly died into a *groan.* It all meant the same thing   We are glad he is going to leave

Aug 16th   We can scarcely keep warm under two blankets these nights   The Chaplain came back this eve also John Boothe and Wm Parker   Gen Banks and Stonewell Jackson have had a bloody fight on the Shenandoah in Va with heavy losses on both sides.[26]

Aug 17th Sunday   The Chaplain preached at 11 o'clock

Aug 18th   A salute was fired in honor of Martin Van Buren — Ex President who has just died   Had a General Muster and this evening we have orders to prepare the usual "two days rations" and to be ready to march at 6 A. M tomorrow

Camp at Hardeman Springs Tennessee

Aug 19th   This morning at 7 o'clock we started south and traveled about five miles and halted at some celebrated springs called Hardemans   Soon an order came for Lieut Hanks and 22 men to go 2½ miles and guard some *cotton*[27]   Fifteen of us were left in camp but were afterwards detailed on Picket and were posted ¾ of a mile out

Aug 20th   We were up at cock-crowing this morning and pumped several

[26] Probably the Battle of Cedar Mountain near Culpeper, Virginia, Aug. 9, 1862. See Williams, *Lincoln Finds a General,* 1:266–72.

[27] "Among other embarrassments . . . was the fact that the government wanted to get out all the cotton possible from the South and directed me to give every facility toward that end. Pay in gold was authorized, and stations on the Mississippi River and on the railroad had to be designated where cotton would be received. This opened to the enemy not only the means of converting cotton into money, which had a value all over the world and which they so much needed, but it afforded them means of obtaining accurate and intelligent information in regard to our position and strength. It was also demoralizing to the troops. Citizens obtaining permits from the treasury department had to be protected within our lines and given facilities to get out cotton by which they realized enormous profits. Men who had enlisted to fight the battles of their country did not like to be engaged in protecting a traffic which went to the support of an enemy they had to fight. . . ." Grant, *Personal Memoirs,* 1:399-400.

cows dry before the owners were out of bed We filled a large kittle full of ripe peaches and with our sugar we had a good long old breakfast Went back to the Springs and established ourselves there There are *five* separate and distinct Springs here and each of them said to be a different kind of water One is sulphur and one Iron and the others are different All said to possess valuable medical properties

A building in octagonal shape surrounds each spring On the steep hill side is a long string of log and frame buildings designed as Hotel, Bath Rooms &c for the convenience of persons attending the place An old Negro who was a servant here told us it was a great place for *de* gemmen to *bab* pleasure But said he *dey* take no pleasure hereabouts *now* The water boils up above the top of the basins and is cold and clear while all around are large and handsome shade trees and the ground all covered with a beautiful carpet of grass. There is a Ball alley here and the men make constant use of it

Aug 21st Weather fine Took a good bath this morning Several of us went out and got all the peaches we wanted and the very finest too. No men are at home through this country They are in the Southern army The boys brought in a lot of chickens to-day Old Sergt Gray is the champion *forager* of the Regt and Co When Gray cannot find fresh meat it is of no use for any other man to look. . .

Aug 22d The Buildings here are being taken for Hospitals and all the sick are being brought from Bolivar Went out to forage a little this afternoon While coming in saw some teams making for camp with all the speed that could be got out of the mule teams The drivers were *lashing* and pounding the mules and making *splendid* time The teamster yelled at us and said the Rebs were coming down on us When we came to camp we could not hear anything more about the Rebs

Aug 23d An order came to us this morning to allow no man to leave camp as an attack by the enemy was expected at any moment. The suspicion was excited by the fact that there was a large meeting of the *Secesh* at Bolivar this afternoon and some treachery may be anticipated

Aug 24th Sunday. 28 of Co "G" were out on Picket to-day News comes that Genl McClellan has *crawfished* from the Peninsula Brig Genl McClernand is here now [28]

[28] Maj.-Gen. John A. McClernand had been given command of the troops in this area on June 24, 1862. *Official Records*, Series I, Vol. XVII, Part II, 31.

Contrabands (a new name for the Negro slaves) are building forts around here and falling trees across the roads to keep the enemies cavalry from surprising us A good many soldiers and people are *bitterly* opposed to having "Niggers" take any hand in this War I am not one of those kind of people If a *culled* man will dig trenches and chop down timber and even fight the enemy he is just the fellow we want and the sooner we recognize this the quicker the war will *end*. . .

Aug 26th Weather fine and clear On Picket. A large foraging expedition composed of the 16th Ia which has been gone four or five days returned last evening and brought back with them 400 "contrabands" 30 mules, 12 wagons and a large amount of other Captures. This morning the camp was alive with colored men women and children hunting situations in the Brigade as cooks or any kind of servants for "*de* Union boys" Our Company took three big strong darkies to cook But one of them ran away before noon and the other two look as if they would run any time They were too much *overjoyed* at the idea of being *free* and well they may be. . .

Camp at Bolivar Tennessee
Aug 29th Left the Springs (much to our regret) and came back to Bolivar The road was awful dusty and we had rather a tough time getting in When we arrived the news had come that 6000 cavalry supposed to be the advance guard of Price's army from the Southwest were advancing upon us. The rumor may be true but I do not believe it These stories are getting to be too common

Aug 30 This afternoon there was a big *scare* and grave rumors that an attack was momentarily expected We were warned by a despatch from Corinth that 6000 Rebel Cavalry were coming down on this point At Noon the assembly beat and we fell into line with the inevitable 40 rounds and canteens filled with water We marched through Bolivar in quick time with the dust six inches deep and the temperature at about 100° in the shade The men women and children stood in groups about the houses with a look of anxiety contempt and scorn as we passed by

On we went through clouds of dust so dense that we could not see one rod ahead Halted south of town about one Mile by which time we were about *gone up* with thirst and heat Loaded guns. A squad of our Cavalry came down the road on which we were placed under full *gallop* and Col

Reid counter marched us We went back ¼ of a mile and tore down a
fence and marched into a corn field Here we laid on the ground ½ hour
and then we marched back again into the lane and toward camp ½ a mile
and formed again in line of *battle* By this time the sun had set and *no
blood been shed* except four or five wounded cavalrymen who were brought
in this evening[29]

Aug 31st Sunday About 2 o'clock this morning Col Reid came "whis-
pering" around the tents and *warned* the men to be prepared to *fight* In a
short time the most of us in line went to sleep and slept until morning We
had no blankets with us and our bed was in an old Rye field We just
wallowed around in the dirt and slept "bully" The field on which we slept
was on the farm of Edwin Polk who is a nephew of the deceased President
Polk and the said Edwin Polk Esq being absent from his agricultural occupation — took a hand in the fracas at Shiloh and came out a prisoner
with the loss of one *leg* His house a large frame building was deserted and
wagon loads of Papers were scattered around over the plantation

Cavalry from the front report the enemy about five miles away and
camped on a creek I was sent back to camp to gather up some provisions
but had only got there when the Regt came in Dr Gibbons our Surgeon
came in from the front and says no enemy is near us He saw Lieut Col
Hoag of 2d Ills Cavalry with *seven* bullet holes through his body and the
hogs had eaten nearly all the face off[30] He also found one of our men and
one of the enemy wounded The Rebs had 500 mounted men Sixty-five
men of the 20th Ohio were captured yesterday Col Reid commanded our
Brigade and Col Crocker the Post Railroad torn up and the telegraph lines
cut all around Thus ended this miserable affair Had to make out several
Reports and Muster Rolls to-day

Sept 1st Reveille at 5½ o'clock this morning. Had the men out in
quick time with Arms. Were ordered to cook and eat breakfast and to be
ready to march immediately But after all we did not March These false
alarms and orders and *counter orders* wear men out but I suppose we are

[29] The 15th Iowa evidently was too late at this engagement to be of much use.
Actually, the "skirmish" lasted about 7 hours, from about 9 in the morning until 4
in the afternoon, in which about 900 Union troops met and drove off an attack of
6,000 Confederates, with a loss of 5 men killed, 18 wounded, and 64 missing. *Official Records*, Series I, Vol. XVII, Part I, 45–9.

[30] Colonel Harvey Hogg had been killed leading a charge of cavalry on Aug. 30.
Ibid., 48.

here to be worn out or put to any use the officers see fit Heavy cannon-ading all the forenoon in the direction of Toombs station[31]

Sept 2d At 1 oclock this morning I was awakened by the noise of wagons and teams and the busy hum of voices in camp But concluded I would take another *nap* before Reveille At 3 o'clock drums beat and we were hurried up to learn that the Rebel Genl Sterling Price[32] (formerly of Missouri) would perhaps *attempt* to take *breakfast* with us with 30,000 of his *friends* who were along with him and not being prepared to accom-modate so many at a regular meal we might be able by early rising to *dish* them up something as they were reported to be *seven* miles way We packed Knapsacks and had tents and baggage all loaded in the wagons by sun up and were ready for anything But no "further orders" until 9 o'clock when we were started from our old camp and went out near one of the forts which had two guns Co "B" and "A" were thrown out as Pickets or skirmishers. Here were all the wagons and Baggage of the Brigade down in a *hollow* From here we were marched behind a heavy embankment near the Railroad — stacked arms and broke ranks

Lieut Hanks said it looked like we were going to *surrender* and I noticed two or three big *tears* in his eyes as he whispered to some of us News came to us that Bolivar had [been] *surrendered* by the troops there The enemy was said to be 30,000 strong Many of the officers looked pale and depressed about this time The contrabands were also *panic* stricken and one or two hundred were running around and most of them women and loaded down with old beds, cooking utensils and old traps of no use to any body. We were supposed to have about 6,500 men and could make a good show for a fight even if we were outnumbered Horses, mules, sut-lers, niggers were all mixed up and jamed into the hollow we were a hard looking crowd anyway

Evening The *panic* is over and we now understand that the large force thought to be around here existed more in the imagination than any place

[31] Col. E. S. Dennis of the 30th Illinois, with the 20th Illinois, two companies of cavalry, and two pieces of artillery—in all some 800 men—was attacked by seven cavalry regiments, consisting of about 5,000. After about a four-hour battle, Col. Dennis remained in possession of the field, with 5 dead, while the enemy retired with a loss of 400 killed and wounded. *Ibid.*, 50.

[32] Maj.-Gen. Sterling Price had been given command of the Confederate Army of the West on July 3, 1862. On July 21, Bragg, in command of the Confederate Dis-trict No. 2, ordered the Army of the Mississippi to Chattanooga, and placed Price in

else   The Railroad has been torn up toward Jackson and a hard fight in which over one hundred of the enemy were killed   Put up our tents and camped

Sept 3d   Our camp is in an old field and the weeds are higher than a mans head and no shade   Water quarter of a mile off   General Crocker says this is where he wants us and here we will stay

Sept 4th   Weather hot   The men have been engaged all day fixing up shade around their tents digging wells sinks &c   Good news from Va   Rebs defeated at Manassas[33]. . .

Sept 7th Sunday   Men have been kept on works and Picket all day Weather hot as usual   Capt Cunningham has been elected Major of the Regiment   Major Belknap is Lieut Col   Lieut Hanks told us this evening to hold an election for Capt and 2d [Lieut.]   The Knoxville men hung together and elected Hanks Capt and Wm Cathcart 2d Lieut   The boys run me against Cathcart   The latter received 33 votes and myself 30   Cathcart was declared *elected*   I am deeply disappointed for I have had the most vexatious and laborious place in the Company and because I can do the work and others can dodge their own duties I shall be *kept* where I am   All right   some men care more for money and position than they do for the government   W. T Cunningham managed the election and is better up to *tricks* than I am   If I had made any effort to get the office I could have had it.   Not over fifteen minutes was given as notice of the election   Besides by the right of rank and in the regular line of promotion the place was mine.   I can only quietly submit but I shall not *forget*

Sept 8th   Weather hot and cloudy   I have been in a bad humor all day caused by the knowledge of the way some of the men in this Company have acted and who pretend to be my best *friends*   I have been slain in the house of these same *friends*   Orders have come this evening to prepare to march.

Sept 9th   Orders came late last night and I was up almost all night

command of the District of the Tennessee. *Ibid.*, 2. The excitement of this day at the Union camp near Bolivar, Tennessee, some twenty miles north of Corinth, is indicative of the prevalence of unfounded rumors; Price, at this time, was some fifty miles south of Corinth, at Tupelo, Mississippi, awaiting help from Maj.-Gen. Earl Van Dorn before moving north toward Iuka and Corinth. *Ibid.*, 121.

[33] A premature account of victory at the Second Battle of Bull Run, which was later turned into a defeat for the Union forces. Williams, *Lincoln Finds a General*, 1:309–355.

drawing rations and seeing that the men were properly prepared for marching Lieut Hanks took me out and privately told me that he never was so disappointed in his life that I had not been elected 2d Lieut and that he was bound to have the place for me yet I cannot quite *swallow this fish* This evening there was a *mock prayer meeting* in Co "K" They sang and prayed in blasphemous mockery This work ought to be stoped by the officers — but they only *laughed*. . .

Sept 11th. . . This evening we have orders to be ready to move at daylight to-morrow morning We will perhaps go to Corinth The whole Brigade is included

On the march in Tennessee

Sept 12th Started early and marched south through Bolivar and back the way we came By evening we had reached the little Hatchie and on about one mile — and then countermarched back to the River and camped in an old field Had sweet potatoes for supper Many of the men *pegged out* to-day as the heat and dust was very oppressive

Sept 13th We had a hard march to-day The heat was so excessive and the dust deep. Are camped tonight on the west bank of the Tuscumbia river We found plenty of roasting ears and *Paw-paws* Genl Crocker who commands is very strict and gave command to allow no man to leave ranks for a moment unless from necessity and then his nearest man must carry his gun and other equipment until he returns Major Purcell who had charge of the rear guard captured one of our drummers who was getting some peaches and the Major tied him to a wagon and marched him along like a gov't mule until night To-night we are all very weary and will lie down on the ground and sleep soundly

Sept 14th Sunday Started on the march at break of day Company "G" in advance as guard At noon we came to the Picket line of the garrison at Corinth then we fell back to our place in the Regiment There was no water on the road from the river we left this morn and the heat was terrible Men began to drop out of the ranks and no rear guard or officer could make them keep up No water could be found When near Corinth we turned south down into an old field in a low place and *oh how hot* I was almost blind from headache and thirst Fully one half the men were *missing* Many fell from *sun stroke* and died on the ground Halted about one hour when orders came to march east of Corinth 4 miles and go into camp This we proceeded to accomplish But as the sun went down and darkness began to come on the men kept falling out They lay like swine in the fence corners and under the bushes or behind logs or any place to *rest* The Regt dwindled down to a Company and almost all the officers were in ambulances or on horses. Finaly we halted and but 14 men of Co "G" were left and there would have been but 13 if we had gone any farther

Sergt Gray, Dan and I lay down by a tree about as much *dead* as alive Gray giving one parting *cuss* at the officers on *horseback* We had not more than closed our weary eyes when Gray gave a whoop and yelled out to some fellow who had lain down by him — and wanted to know who he was The fellow spoke and soon as we heard his voice we knew it was a *darkey* Gray swore at him in both english and Mexican and told him to travel — and travel he did

Sept 15th Some of the men did not get up until noon to-day Hanks and Cathcart were both behind Have put up our tents. Went over to Corinth to-day. We have orders to march at day break to-morrow

March on Juka Mississippi

Sept 16th Have traveled all day and toward all points of the compass and the rain has poured down all the time turning the dust all to mud. Have been in a dense forest of oak and pine most of the time We are wet to the hide and the air is very cold Went into Camp or rather bivouac about dark. We made up a fire in some old pine logs and stayed up most of the night drying our clothes and keeping warm The rain has ceased

Sept 17th Last night about 2 o'clock the rain came down again in torrents and compelled us to get up and stand by the fire the bal of the night Weather to-day cool and cloudy Have traveled all day through a country not inhabited and full of swamps We are in Alabama and tonight are camped within 2 miles of Price's Army said to be 25,000 strong at a place called Iuka. . .[34]

Camp at Juka Mississippi

Sept 19th Started early this morning with 100 rounds each Came within sight of the Rebel pickets about 9 o'clock and formed in line of battle and with skirmishers thrown out advanced through an almost impenetrable thicket of young pines from three to ten feet high The ground was very hilly The skirmishers kept up a brisk fire and Co "A" shot one

[34] Iuka, Mississippi, is close to the Alabama boundary; possibly the 15th Iowa crossed the border into the latter state during their advance.

THE BATTLE OF SHILOH

CYRUS F. BOYD

HUGH T. REID

WILLIAM W. BELKNAP

JOHN MACARTHUR

DANIEL EMBREE

THE BATTLE OF CORINTH—Storming Battery Robinette

of our own Cavalrymen horse and laid the rider off on the ground   We laid in line of battle all day and will sleep on our arms to-night [35]

Sept 20th   Advanced toward Iuka this morning and entered the town at noon and found the enemy had *skedaddled* cutting his way through Rosecrans right wing and escaping to the South   Where they cut through about one mile and one half from here there was a desperate contest and some of our regiments have suffered severely   The 5th Iowa lost a great many men killed   The large Hotel here is already full of wounded Rebs.   Most of them belong to Texas regiments   There are about 400 wounded here   Many of them are badly hurt and say if they can only get home they will fight no more   Some of them were deranged and looked horrible as they raved and rolled in their blood   Some had their legs and some their arms amputated   Most of them had lain on the field since the evening before   The women of Iuka seemed very attentive to all their wants   Saw one large Texan wounded badly and I think he would die but he was pluck to the core.   I talked to him awhile   He took a large minnie ball from his vest pocket and showed me   The ball was flattened and he said he got that in his hip last spring at *Shiloh* from the *"Yanks"* and now he had another in him — but said he expected to be up again and as soon as he could he would be after us again.   I said "Bully for you old boy" and bid him good bye. . .

[35] Price had moved from the railroad south of Corinth northeast toward Iuka, some twenty miles east of Corinth, intending to join Bragg, who was racing toward the Ohio River. Buell and his Army of the Ohio were also moving toward the Ohio River, to cut off Bragg. Grant's forces were concentrated at Memphis (W. T. Sherman), Bolivar (Ord), and Corinth (Rosecrans). To save his army and protect Buell, Grant had to save Iuka. Ord, from Bolivar, was ordered to the north of Iuka; Rosecrans from Corinth moved to the south, thus hemming Price at Iuka. Both were to move on Sept. 19, Ord to the north when he heard Rosecrans' guns to the south. However, because of an adverse wind, Ord did not hear the attack commence, and thus Rosecrans bore the burden of the fighting on the 19th. When Rosecrans prepared to resume the attack on the morning of the 20th Price had withdrawn and escaped. The 15th Iowa, held in reserve under Ord, did not take part in this battle. For details of the Battle of Iuka, see Grant, *Personal Memoirs*, 1:403–413; *Official Records*, Series I, Vol. XVII, Part I, 60–137; S. H. M. Byers, *Iowa in War Times* (Des Moines, 1888), 149–58.

PART III

IUKA TO LAFAYETTE, TENNESSEE

September 22, 1862 to December 31, 1862

The Battle of Corinth

[Iuka, Mississippi]

Sept 22nd [1862] Weather hot. Went out to some Rebel Camps to-day and brought in a lot of Tents which we needed very much The 37th Ala must have lost all their camp equipage as we found everything in good shape and took it for the use of the "Yanks" Have put up our tents down in a low bottom on the north side of the Railroad and in a most unhealthy place The green-flies are so thick here that the earth can scarcely be seen in many spots and they hang in the bushes like bees in swarming time

Sept 29th Since the 22d nothing of note has transpired The weather continues hot With one or two others I went to look at the battle-field Where the enemy cut through our lines there has been most severe fighting. I have never seen before evidence of such a desperate contest on a small piece of ground The fight was for the possession of a field battery and was on the crest of a hill in the timber The trees around are almost torn to kindling wood by the dreadful fire of the Artillery and Musketry. 25 dead horses lay close together and about 40 men belonging to the 5th Iowa Inft buried in *one grave* here. Besides numerous other graves scattered all through the woods Many of the 17th Iowa were killed[1] Saw many of the enemies dead lying around not more than half covered The ground in many places was *white* as snow with *creeping worms* The darkness of the forest and the terrible mortality made it one of the most *horrible* places I was ever in Then the *silence* was oppressive Not a sound could be heard

---

[1] Iowa losses were heavy at Iuka. The 5th Iowa lost 217 killed, wounded, and missing or captured; the 10th lost 7; the 16th, 75; the 17th, 46; and the 2nd Cavalry, 6. *The War of the Rebellion: A Compilation of the Official Records of the Union and Confederate Armies . . .*, Series I, Vol. XVII, Part I, 78. (Hereafter referred to as *Official Records.*)

except once in a while the chirp of some lonely bird in the deep forest To
think of our poor fellows left to sleep in that dark wood (But one must not
think of such things) . . .

Forced march to Corinth Mississippi

Oct 1st We were called up at 11 oclock last night and ordered to be
ready to march immediately[2] Got ready but did not start until daylight
Came 20 miles to-day and within 6 miles of Corinth Cathcart received his
commission yesterday and to-day took his place in the Company as 2d
Lieut Our men set fire to all the houses along the line of march to-day I
think this is wrong and should [be] stoped at once

Oct 2d Arrived in Corinth about 10 o'clock. Went two miles west of
town and camped. . . . Corinth is well fortified now and is surrounded by
forts and abatis or fallen timber along all the roads.

Battle of Corinth Miss[3]

Oct 3d At break of day we were called up by the drums and fell into
Companies thinking that the weather was hot we were going out to drill
before breakfast as had been our habit in hot weather With the whole
Brigade we marched North about one mile through the woods. Were arranged in line of battle and stacked arms and while here a detail went back
to camp and brought up some breakfast About 9 oclock rumor came that
Price and Van Dorn were marching on Corinth and we should perhaps
have a fight But few believed the story. By 10 o'clock the sound of artillery and musketry could be heard to the west about as far away as Chewalla The noise of the guns became nearer and by 1 o'clock we could see
masses of the enemy marching along the Memphis and Charleston Railroad
to the west The troops in front of us kept falling back and finaly took

[2] Since the retreat of Confederate General Sterling Price from Iuka to Baldwyn,
Mississippi, he and Major-General Earl Van Dorn had been gathering their troops
for an assault on Grant's position at Corinth. "By the 1st of October it was fully
apparent that Corinth was to be attacked with great force and determination, and
that Van Dorn, Lovell, Price, Villepique and Rust had joined their strength for
this purpose." *Personal Memoirs of U. S. Grant* (2 vols., New York, 1885), 1:415-
16. According to Sherman, Grant had only about 50,000 men under him at this
time, "to defend a frontage of a hundred and fifty miles, guard some two hundred
miles of railway, and as much river." On the other side, Van Dorn had 40,000
men, could concentrate them at any point on Grant's long line, and attack through
country they knew well. *Memoirs of Gen. W. T. Sherman* . . . (2 vols., New York,
1891), 1:290.

[3] For William W. Belknap's and Marcellus M. Crocker's accounts of the 15th
Iowa in this battle, see *Official Records*, Series I, Vol. XVII, Part I, 358–62, 363–5.

position in line to our right The 11th and 13th [Iowa] were posted a little way behind us as a Reserve

We occupied a naked high ridge with nothing to protect us from the fire of the enemy About 2 oclock we could see them advancing toward our position in line of battle There were three distinct lines one behind the other and all advancing in the most deliberate manner at *bayonets fixed* We could hear the commands of the Rebel Officers distinctly, but we were cautioned "not to fire until we received orders to open" Genl Crocker and Lieut Col Belknap rode along the line and urged no man to fire until the order was given [4]

Our men got upon one knee and had guns all cocked and ready when the front Regiments of the enemy took deliberate aim at us and the whole line fired into us and we heard the Rebel shout and *yell* Then somebody commenced firing and we shot away in the smoke not knowing exactly where to aim as the enemy were in lower ground than we But their first volley laid out many a man for us Every one now took to a tree or some place to protect himself The Rebs soon closed upon us and came on with countless numbers They swarmed around on our left and fired from behind trees and logs and kept pressing forward Our ranks became much confused and the regiments held as a Reserve fell back toward our Camp without helping us any

The battle raged fiercely for a time and men fell in great numbers Middlesworth the 1st Corporal in our company stood at my left hand and a ball struck him in the abdomen and he fell with a groan — Corp Heatley fell shot through the head and Lieut Cathcart fell dead at almost the first fire He had on his sword and uniform Several of our Company were wounded and the enemy closing in so rapidly the whole Regiment began to fall back not having even time to pick up the wounded but left them to their *fate* Just as the Regt began to break Charley Vinton came staggering along by me and asked some fellow who passed him to help him The man

[4] That the officers might experience the same feelings as the private soldiers would probably have surprised the men at Corinth. William W. Belknap tells a story of the battle of Corinth: "General [then Colonel] Crocker said to me at Corinth, in the very heat of the fight, as a bullet struck 'spat' on the sapling between us: 'Do you know, old fellow, what I am thinking about?' 'What, colonel?' said I. 'I wish I was back in Des Moines.' And so did I wish myself back in Keokuk." William W. Belknap, "The Obedience and Courage of the Private Soldier . . .," *War Sketches and Incidents . . . Iowa Commandery, Military Order of the Loyal Legion . . .* (2 vols., Des Moines, 1893), 1:165.

did not stop or take any notice whatever of him and I took Charley by the arm and assisted him for some distance He was wounded not severely in the head but the blood covered him all over and he looked like one mortally wounded I left him with a Surgeon who was trying to get some other wounded men to an ambulance

To our left I could now see the Rebs running from tree to tree and firing rapidly while our men were doing the same but falling back toward the Camp The tents had been lowered to the ground and the volleys of bullets did not hurt them I could see the Rebs tearing the Sutlers tents away and going for the goods I fired nine or ten rounds all told and by this time everything was on the *retreat* toward Corinth and the fireing had almost ceased in the woods We were outside the abatis and all the roads leading in toward Corinth were crowded with men hurrying toward the town When we reached the timber inside the abatis it was almost sun-down Here we formed another line of battle and under cover of Fort Williams[5] The men kept straggling in for an hour and some did not come in at all Sam Roberts, Henry Hooten and Clark were missing and must have been taken prisoners Here we lie, on our arms for the night under a clear sky

Oct 4th The enemy could be heard all night bringing up his artillery and the rolling of wheels and the commands of the officers could be distinctly heard A little before daylight a Rebel shell came from a gun in the edge of the wood and went over into the town — another soon followed and soon the cannonade opened in good earnest Our Fort opened on a Rebel battery and soon silenced its fire Several shells came over to wake us up and a number of men in the 11th Iowa just in rear of us were wounded[6]

[5] Corinth was surrounded by six outer batteries, numbers "A" to "F"—and by seven inner batteries or forts—Powell, Robinette, Williams, Phillips, Tannrath, Lothrop, and Madison. By the night of Oct. 3, Confederate troops had pushed in to this second line of fortifications. The 15th Iowa had been driven back from Battery F—north and west of Corinth—to Fort Phillips, not Williams, as Boyd states, although the two batteries were very close. For maps of the battle, see *Official Records*, Atlas, Vol. I, Plate XXV-1 and Plate XXIII-9, 10. A witness of the battle, writing in the Des Moines *Register*, credits Rosecrans with brilliant strategy in this retreat, whereby he brought the Confederate forces closer to the "heavy guns of the inner fortifications." Des Moines *Iowa State Register*, Oct. 29, 1862. According to Grant, Rosecrans withdrew, awaiting reinforcements which were coming from Jackson and Bolivar. Grant, *Personal Memoirs*, 1:416-17. Rosecrans' report does not give any indication of such a strategem. *Official Records*, Series I, Vol. XVII, Part I, 166–70.

[6] A newspaper description of this artillery duel is more dramatic than Boyd's account: "Under cover of night the rebels had the temerity to plant a battery

Fort Williams contains 5, 34 and 64 pounders and she put some heavy shells over into the woods which must have made havoc among the enemy We were warned to lie close to the ground and look out for a *charge* Fort Robinette on our right and distant about 400 yards kept up a heavy fire upon the woods in front the enemy answering occasionally

About 10 o'clock a heavy roll of musketry was heard to the North and looking over in front of Robinette we could see thousands of gray uniforms swarming from the woods and climbing over the fallen timber Every one came as best he could toward the works The cannon at Robinette poured charge after charge into their ranks but they faltered not and on they came and soon reached the work[s] The gunners stood to their pieces and many of them *fell there* A few ran back to the rear where the Infantry lay about 200 yards from the fort. The "Stars and bars" floated over Robinette but only for a brief time of a few seconds. The Infantry rose from their lair and with fixed and glistening bayonets and one discharge from their muskets rushed on the victorious legions [and] with a *cheer* killed or captured all that were left No sooner had the smoke cleared away than the second assaulting force emerged from the woods and bore down on Robinette with the most *terrific yells* The guns from the fort loaded with grape and canister mowed them down by hundreds But when the advance had almost reached the fort the gunners this time abandoned their pieces and ran back to the Infantry. The Rebs headed by an officer who had come up a winding road on horseback now reached the redoubt and began climbing over its walls and some ran around the embankment and got possession of the guns and had them *turned* on our men when a long *blue* line of uniforms could be seen rising out of the grass and bushes and with a *cheer* rushed on the victorious enemy Muskets were clubbed and many were killed with the bayonet The ranks of the rebels melted like snow and most of them stood their ground and died in and around the little fort

within 200 yards of the west redoubt; and at 3½ A. M. commenced shelling the town. This discovered their position and then began one of the most splendid artillery duels ever witnessed. Every gun that could get range opened its heavy bay on the devoted little battery. The terrific thunder of the artillery shook the whole surrounding country. No words of mine can describe the awful grandeur of the scene, as the crashing solid shot and screaming shells went flying through the air. This cannonading lasted until daybreak, when a sortie was made from the redoubt and the artillery dragged back in triumph. All this time we lay flat on our faces and were scarcely allowed to move. An awful stillness succeeded this cannonade; for more than hour not a sound was heard." Letter from R. K. Miller in *Des Moines Iowa State Register*, Oct. 29, 1862.

It was a bloody contest and we could see men using their bayonets like pitch forks, and thrusting each other through How glorious the old flag looked as it again floated over the works in the smoke and breath of battle

Finaly those of the enemy who did not fall or surrender started for the woods across the abatis or by the meandering roads for the shelter of the timber It was every fellow for himself and the "devil take the hindmost" No description is adequate to picture the gauntlet of death that these fugitives ran. Very few reached the timber *alive* Robinette belched forth her fearful burden of shell and grape in their rear and our fort threw in a flanking fire of heavy shell while a field battery between us and Robinette raked the bal[ance] of the ground and the Infantry poured after them a deadly rain of musket balls

With no guns and coats and hats gone I saw a scattering few reach the timber and escape from the "jaws of death" Although they are enemies of our government and our flag I could not help but *pity* these poor fellows who thus went into *certain* and *sure destruction* here When the smoke had cleared away we learned that the enemy had fled in confusion They had been *cut to pieces* in the most intense meaning of that term. Such bravery has never been excelled on any field as the useless assaults on Robinette[7] The prisoners tell us that Van Dorn commanded and that he was *drunk* and ordered his men to drink whiskey and *gun powder* and then ordered them to take the works at any cost *however great*[8]

In front of Robinette lie hundreds of dead. 126 dead men lie within 40 feet of the fort. Most of them are in the ditch surrounding One dead man

[7] Admiration for the fighting qualities of the Confederates was general, from Grant to the privates of the Union army. The "gallantry" of the troops under Price was commented on in practically every report. "Let no intelligent man call the rebels cowards. In the engagement they displayed a desperate courage seldom equalled and never surpassed. For a battalion to rush upon a redoubt filled with blazing-throated artillery and planting the flag, hold it there till riddled by a thousand balls, while double charged field pieces from our center hurled canister and death into their right flank, is worthy to be compared with any charge recorded in history." Letter from R. K. Miller in Des Moines *Iowa State Register*, Oct. 29, 1862. Of the first charge, on October 3, a member of the 17th Iowa wrote: "An involuntary acclamation of admiration burst from our entire Brigade on beholding the gallantry and daring of the [Confederate] charge." Keokuk *Gate City*, Oct. 15, 1862.

[8] Van Dorn was tried by a Confederate Court of Inquiry at Jackson, Mississippi, on November 7, 1862, charged with drunkenness and neglect of duty at the Battle of Corinth. The Court found him innocent of the many charges against him. *Official Records*, Series I, Vol. XVII, Part I, 414–59.

lies just on the slope of the work stiff in death with a hammer in one hand and a lot of *rat tail files* in the other His mission had been to *spike the cannon* They are so tightly gripped that the fingers can scarcely be opened Several others I saw with their muskets *gripped* in their dead hands as tight as a vise could hold Thus they perished with the most unearthly look on their dying faces Col Rogers of a Texas Regt who led the charge lies dead with his slain horse within a few feet of the fort and his Adjt only a few yards from him All around them were heaps of slain — principaly Texas and Arkansas men

Price, Van Dorn, Villepique and all the transmissipi troops were here and it was one last desperate effort to retrieve their losses in the Missippi Valley But this is the worst set back they have met. . . .

Have orders to be ready to march at daylight tomorrow morning Genl Rosecrans our commanding General came around this eve and was almost taken from his horse by the soldiers The *wildest enthusiasm* prevailed and every man seems ready to pursue the enemy We have had but few battles so well managed as old "Rosa" has managed this one

The dead have been burried this eve and we did not even get to see those of our Regiment as details from other Regiments burried them Some of the enemy penetrated into the town and more than 100 were captured in the *bakeries* and *stores* We are tired and hungry to-night and the excitement and fatigue of the two days battle and its glorious termination entitles us to a *rest*

Oct 5th Sunday. Started toward Chewalla early this morning in pursuit of the flying enemy The roadside for miles was lined with abandoned wagons [and] dead and wounded Rebs who had been left in the *retreat* of yesterday Saw sixteen dead in one place They lay like sheaves of grain ready to be shocked and all along the road we found them The panic has been an awful one Went six miles and formed in line of battle and here we remained two hours Genl McArthur commands [9] Finaly started on and came within two miles of the Tuscumbia River and on the same road which brought us to and from Bolivar Here we bivouacked

Oct 6th Started early and crossed the Tuscumbia and went South We soon began to see more signs of the *rout* The hills were steep and wagons

[9] Brig.-Gen. John McArthur succeeded Brig.-Gen. Thomas J. McKean in command of the 6th Division of the Army of the Tennessee. See *Dictionary of American Biography*, 11: 551-2; *Official Records*, Series I, Vol. XVII, Part I, 345, 361.

had struck trees and rolled over and over Some had been loaded with Corn meal and some with flour and others with cooking utensils and all kinds of stuff was scattered like some great whirlwind had overtaken the retreating army Artillery caisons had struck trees and the ammunition had exploded tearing everything to pieces around Many places the cannoniers had cut the *traces* and gone leaving their load behind The hillsides were white with corn meal and flour and the dust in the road fully one foot deep [10] Thus for several miles it went. We found Genl Prices *buggy* with a fine Robe in it But the owner had *gone on* All along the roadside under the bushes in the hollows and behind logs the panting fugitives were found Glad to surrender. Glad to do anything to save all they had *left* and that was their *lives* They all agreed in saying that no such *terrible* calamity had ever overtaken [them] in the west as the battle of the 4th

Hurlbut had come down on them at the Hatchie [11] and used them up badly and if we had closed in on them Sunday instead of lying on our arms in the woods there would not have been enough left to *tell the tale* [12]

[10] William H. Warren of the 13th Iowa was in the pursuit. "We followed them up on their retreat and done them greater damage they burnt a part of their train on the Tuscumbia where we were clost on their heals gineral ord [General E. O. C. Ord] headed them on the Hatchie as we drove them through thare and cut them up badly the road was strued with tents waggons and clothing knapsacks shugar molases flower and corn meal besides cooking utentials, canon carriage and amunition and guns. I did not see enny canon but it was reported that our scouts found ten peaces of canon throed into a gulley one half mile off the road." Letter of October 12, 1862, Wm. H. Warren to his wife, in *Warren Letters* (typescript), State Historical Society of Iowa, Iowa City.

[11] Maj.-Gen. Stephen A. Hurlbut, in command of the Fourth Division of the Army of West Tennessee, had been ordered from Bolivar to support Rosecrans at Corinth. Maj.-Gen. E. O. C. Ord "had joined Hurlbut on the 4th and being senior took command of his troops. This force encountered the head of Van Dorn's retreating column just as it was crossing the Hatchie by a bridge some ten miles out from Corinth. The bottom land here was swampy and bad for the operations of troops, making a good place to get an enemy into. Ord attacked the troops that had crossed the bridge and drove them back in a panic. Many were killed, and others were drowned by being pushed off the bridge in their hurried retreat." Grant, *Personal Memoirs*, 1:417-18. See also *Official Records*, Series I, Vol. XVII, Part I, 304–335.

[12] "General Rosecrans . . . failed to follow up the victory, although I had given specific orders in advance of the battle for him to pursue the moment the enemy was repelled. He did not do so, and I repeated the order after the battle. . . . Rosecrans did not start in pursuit till the morning of the 5th and then took the wrong road. Moving in the enemy's country he travelled with a wagon train to carry his provisions and munitions of war. His march was therefore slower than that of the enemy, who was moving towards his supplies. Two or three hours of pursuit on the day of battle, without anything except what the men carried on

Six miles more brought us to the Hatchie River and the fleeing enemy had burned the bridge behind him and here we were compelled to stop until it is repaired

Oct 7th   Crossed the Hatchie and went in after the *Secesh* But they had the start and we only once came up with their rear *guard* They made a show of fight and detained us an hour or two until the main force could get ahead again We captured a few prisoners. Are within two miles of Ripley to-night Weather rainy and wet

Oct 8th   We have been idle all day Have been hunting sweet potatoes as these are all we have to eat besides a little fresh meat we found. . . . The inhabitants of the land have all fled and forsaken home and attachments. . . .

March to Corinth Mississippi

Oct 10th   The pursuit has closed Marched toward Corinth to-day at 2 o'clock [13] The rain was pouring down and Co "G" was detailed as *rear guard* We had a hard time Came through Ripley a town (when the people are at home) of about 600 inhabitants The mud was deep and the wind blew cold from the North When we halted this evening the rain was pouring down and we are wet through and mud from head to foot. Are burning some chestnut rails to-night to dry our clothes

Oct 11th   Had no blankets with us and we suffered much last night in the cold rain We could not sleep and had to stand up about all night around a little fire which we tried to keep alive Have reached the Hatchie and are camped on the North bank We have made good time to-day

Oct 12th   Weather fine Crossed the Tuscumbia about noon Rested

their persons, would have been worth more than any pursuit commenced the next day could have possibly been. Even when he did start, if Rosecrans had followed the route taken by the enemy, he would have come upon Van Dorn in a swamp with a stream in front and Ord holding the only bridge; but he took the road leading north and towards Chewalla instead of west, and, after having marched as far as the enemy had moved to get to the Hatchie, he was as far from battle as when he started." Grant, *Personal Memoirs*, 1:416–19. "General Rosecrans had become favorably known through his operations in northern Mississippi, where he had fought successfully against the Confederate Generals Earl Van Dorn and Sterling Price. In their attack on Corinth, which Rosecrans defended, they had suffered a bloody repulse but had escaped fatal damage through Rosecrans' dilatory pursuit, for which Grant, who was in command of the district, never forgave him." Otto Eisenschiml and Ralph Newman, *The American Iliad* . . . (Indianapolis, 1947), 291.

[13] For Col. Crocker's account of this pursuit and return to Corinth, see *Official Records*, Series I, Vol. XVII, Part I, 361-2.

half an hour and came on towards Corinth and reached that place about sundown Am about *pegged out* and so are all the others

Camp at Corinth Mississippi

Oct 13th Have been fixing camp all day Capt Hanks ordered the Company to hold an Election this eve for a Lieut in place of Cathcart *killed* and also for 1st Sergt I was *nominated* and received the *unanimous* vote of the Co for Lieut not one dissenting voice Dan Embree had 8 majority for 1st sergt against Isaiah Welch. . . .

Oct 16th This has been the most unhappy day of my whole life This morning Capt Hanks pale and trembling in every limb called me to his tent and said he had some bad news for me. That Col Reid had for some cause refused to sign a recommendation for me for Lieut and that he had advised Gov Kirkwood of Iowa to appoint E P Bye of Co "G" — a man who has made it his business to *bake pies* and sell them through the camp and *shinneed* around more than any man in the Co and this too without saying anything to the Company and against all their wishes A *thunderbolt* could not have shocked me more than this news I was completely *stupefied* for a moment and could not believe this could be *true* But when I remembered the man Cunningham and that he was now Major and in close communication with Col Reid I saw through the whole *conspiracy* Co "G" are if anything more excited and indignant than I am and they stand by me to a man and swear they will stay by me to the *end* That they voted for me for Lieut and no other man can or shall have the place Even old uncle Johny Cozad is up and has his bristles elevated and says that the man that takes this place against the wishes of the Company will have a hard road to *travel* Capt Rogers Co "E" told me this eve to fight it out and that Co "E" would stand by us.

Oct 17th . . . The boys talk trouble if the *pie* peddlar is made Lieut

Oct 18th To-day I went to see Col Reid and to ask him *why* he had treated me as I have *heard* Reid said I had always been faithful and had done well But in this case his reason for not recommending me for Lieut was that some one had told him that I had assisted a wounded man in getting off the field in the late battle and said I should have known that this was against *orders* and knowing that I had been guilty of disobedience and he could not do otherwise than he had Was *very sorry* &c &c To say that I was *angry* will not express by feelings and I left the old *liar* and *tyrant* and went straight to the tent of Major Belknap (or Lieut Col) and told him plainly all about the whole affair and he said if there was anything in the world he could do for me he would cheerfully do it and it was a piece of *gross injustice* and he wanted to know who this man "Bye" was I told him that he was a *pie Peddlar* in Co "G"

I find that I have the sympathy of about every man in Regt and their good will too, and especially of Co "G" and this is better than to be Col and be *hated* and *despised* as our Col is As mean and tyrannical as he is I shall get *even* with him before I leave the service I never *cared* much about a Commission until *now* but now I shall have one cost what it may and I shall give Mr "Bye" as *thorny* a road to travel as he has ever seen My influence with the men to-day is twice or ten times that of Hanks or any other Commissioned Officer and Hanks *Knows* it.

Oct 19th Sunday . . . The boys are jubilant this eve as we have heard that Lieut Fisk is released as a prisoner and will soon be with us again The enemy *lost* 2000 killed and wounded in the late battle and our loss about 700 [14] Price is said to be concentrating again at Holly Springs with a large army

Have been in the service just *one year* to-day I thank God for all I have enjoyed and the preservation of my life and also for all the hardships and the *disappointments* I have met. If I had received the Commission and been in poor Cathcarts place it might have been far different on this 1st anniversary. . . .

Oct 21st No passes were granted to-day as the officers are afraid the men will enlist in the Regular Army and leave the Volunteers They have a recruiting sta[tion] in town They need not fear to let *me go*

Oct 22d Capt Hanks tells me this eve that he feels certain I will yet be 1st Lieut I guess this is only to let me *down gradually* . . .

Are ordered to prepare for Review which will be 1½ miles East of Corinth We marched out through a cloud of dust and when we got to the ground we fronted and ordered arms — then shouldered arms opened ranks — Then Genl McArthur and staff approached our right from the front and rode along the line at a brisk trot; then down our rear — then he and his escort took a position 200 yards in front and we were wheeled into Column

[14] The losses in the Battle of Corinth, according to the official records, were 2,520 Union men, killed, wounded, or missing; 2,527 Confederate. *Ibid.*, 176, 383. General Sherman questioned this Confederate figure, claiming that their loss must have been at least 6,000. Sherman, *Memoirs* . . ., 291.

and marched in Review in front of the General and around again to our former position — wheeled from a halt into line again and marched to Camp The dust was awful and our eyes and ears were filled These Reviews are the greatest *bore* of the service There is no end to preparation and everything must be *just so* But the reviewing officer sees nothing but the general appearance of the men and hundreds pass in review before him in a few minutes But it keeps mens minds employed and takes their thoughts from something else I am not feeling well this eve.

Oct 23d . . . Rumor says Price is gathering an army at Holly Springs and will perhaps try us again at Corinth He will be warmly received if he calls here again Bragg has escaped from Buell in Kentucky and is retreating South [15] The times look dark and gloomy and there are no signs of peace on the red sky of War . . .

Oct 26th Sunday. This morning the *snow* covered the ground *one inch* deep and it was very cold indeed About noon the sun thawed the snow off. Some one stole the blanket off Major Cunninghams horse last night and to-day he is hunting for it and says if he can find the man he will have him *severely punished* (I think the man is in Co "G" and one of the B. *boys* said to me to-day or rather asked me if I thought a soldier was as good as an Officers "horse" I told him I thought it was *doubtful*)

Oct 27th Weather cool but the day fine to work Every able bodied man in our Regt has been to work on the fortifications to-day The defences around Corinth are of the most formidable character . . .

Oct 29th . . . Price is reported going south, going north, going East, going in all directions . . .

Oct 31st Had Division Review about one mile southwest. Was not well enough to attend Afternoon was Muster and all had to attend This barbarous way of living I do not like Have 3 sad biscuit at a meal — a little fat bacon and coffee Three of us eat on two plates with one spoon and one knife (a shoe knife) and a sharp stick for a fork We wash our plates about once a week We can hardly get water to cook and wash our faces Every one but the Brigadiers and Major Generals are getting *tired* of the war which now looks like it would end like the Kilkeny cat fight — nothing left but the *tails* . . .

---

[15] This was the battle of Perryville or Chaplin Hills in Kentucky, on October 8, 1862. *Personal Memoirs of P. H. Sheridan* . . . (2 vols., New York, 1888), 1:190ff; *Official Records*, Series I, Vol. XVI, Part I, 1021–1135.

82 CIVIL WAR DIARY OF C. F. BOYD

March to Holly Springs Mississippi

Nov 2d Sunday. Received orders last evening to be ready to March to-morrow morning with *seven* days Rations [16] We did not get started until 3 oclock this afternoon Took the Road towards Bolivar and did not stop until 1 oclock at night and three miles from Tuscumbia River I gave out this evening and had to fall out of ranks but caught up again a few minutes after the Regt halted We made some coffee and with one blanket we laid down on the cold frosty ground Many men gave out and went back to Camp

Nov 3d Started at 7 o'clock this morning and kept steadily on until night I gave out about 4 oclock in the evening. I laid down to rest in a fence corner when Qr Master Higley rode along and saw me and told me to get in one of his wagons — I declined with *thanks* Capt Hanks was sick and rode in an Ambulance

Nov 4th Weather clear and warm and awful dusty By advice of the Dr I rode in ambulance until we came to Grand Junction Got out and marched two miles and camped on a hillside close to Davis Creek More men were run down to-night than I ever saw Stragglers burned vacant houses fences cotton mills and almost everything along the road and our track was visible for miles upon miles by the great mountains of smoke that rolled up from our rear These scalawags and stragglers who fire buildings and burn property unauthorized should be punished with death This evening there was an order to have Roll Call half an hour after going into Camp and all absentees to be put on extra duty if privates and if Non-Commissioned Officers to be reduced to the *ranks*

The country passed over to-day was the best we have seen in Tennessee We are 48 miles from Corinth Troops are coming in here from Bolivar and Jackson and there seems to be concentrating here a large Army

[16] This, according to Grant, was the beginning of the campaign against Vicksburg. Grant was then at his headquarters at Jackson, Tenn., north of Corinth. Holly Springs, his first objective, was west and a little south of Corinth. Union forces held the Mississippi above Memphis, and at New Orleans at its mouth. Vicksburg and Port Hudson were the last Confederate bastions on the river. It would take eight months of bitter fighting and stubborn siege before Vicksburg fell to Grant on July 4, 1863. See Grant, *Personal Memoirs*, 1:422–570; for the 11th Iowa in this campaign, see Olynthus B. Clark (ed.), *Downing's Civil War Diary* . . . (Des Moines, 1916), 80–126; Henry Steele Commager (ed.), *The Blue and the Gray* . . . (2 vols., Indianapolis, 1950), 2:645–84 for personal accounts of the siege. See also *Memoirs of Gen. W. T. Sherman* . . ., 1:332–71.

Grand Junction Tennessee

Nov 5th Have been in camp all day. Foraging parties have been out and brought in sweet potatoes &c . . .

Nov 7th Genl Grant who commands has issued an order punishing with *death* any man who burns a building without authority and the cartriges [*sic*] in our boxes to be *counted* every day and men to be charged 50 cts a piece for all lost or destroyed This latter is to stop the shooting along the road of march . . .

Nov 9th Sunday: Moved camp last evening down on a low flat bottom along the creek A reconnoitering force went south to-day and had a skirmish at Cold Water in which some few men were killed and wounded

Nov 10th Weather good. A foraging party went out to-day and brought in 25 bushels of sweet potatoes, 14 sheep and 12 Hogs . . .

Nov 12th Bye received his commission to-day as Lieut I did not *swear* but Co "G" did that part of it for me He takes his position under peculiar circumstances and he will not see much comfort if he does make more than he did baking *pies* to sell

Nov 13th Several of our men came to the Regiment to-day via Bolivar Our Cavalry are reported in possession of Holly Springs [17]

Nov 14th . . . Preparations seem to be making for a forward movement Our teams took out a foraging party to-day and brought in 12 hogs and 14 beeves We are allowed 6 teams to the Regiment now We have to abandon much stuff which we have carried along heretofore and will enable us to follow the "*Confeds*" much more rapidly than formerly and if we have to run back we can also make *better time* and [not] lose the government so much The Rebel forces are somewhere south of Holly Springs location unknown It is common *talk* that Genl McArthur was *drunk* as a fool the night we came here and that he fell off his horse If true this is a disgrace and a shame

Nov 15th This war is getting to be a stupendous humbug The western army has done all that has been accomplished so far and if no better generals can be found than McClellan and some others there will no victories in the East soon . . . We drew 7 days Rations to-day of hard-tack, bacon,

[17] Colonel Albert L. Lee, 7th Kans. Cavalry, entered Holly Springs at daylight on November 13. He found "a considerable force of cavalry, but they skedaddled." *Official Records*, Series I, Vol. XVII, Part I, 488.

sugar, coffee soap candles salt and a few Irish potatoes A band across the creek plays some beautiful music . . .

Nov 17th Last night the rain fell gently and to-day the ground is very muddy and our camp is quite damp to-night and the rain still patters upon the little tent Teams sent out brought in 18 bushels of sweet potatoes and 4 hogs We have eat out clean about one county since we came here and will soon have to move to new pastures Private foraging is not allowed but Qr Masters can take anything and give a receipt therefor and when the war is *over* if the claimant can prove himself a Union man he will be paid for the property None of them will get anything as the inhabitants are all disunion men. They have forsaken wives and children and cotton plantations and gone after Jeff Davis and his "Confederacy" The country thus far that we have seen is not worth one drop of Yankee blood

Nov 18th The water in the creek and out of which we have to cook and use is getting filthy The 16th Ia is camped just above us on the stream and are the nearest to *swine* of anything we have seen to be called men We have Dress Parade every eve

Nov 19th Last night the rain poured down and flooded our camp and about drowned us out, wetting our clothes and blankets. To day we moved up on the hill on a beautiful piece of ground

Nov 20th Weather clear and cool Slept on the cold damp ground last night or tried to but I did not sleep much Sergt Gray went out foraging yesterday and found the country so well cleaned up that he gave up finding anything until at last he went into a house and seeing a negro woman boiling something over the fire in a large boiler he asked her what she had there Not being disposed to tell Gray took the lid off and found a fine large *turkey* just beginning to cook. Gray not wishing to lose any time grabbed the fowl and started on double quick for camp and the *wench* yelling after him "oh *massa* for de lords sake give up dat turkey" The hot water almost cooked Grays arm from the wrist to the elbow But he did not surrender and brought the fowl safely in and we had it baked in our big *oven* which we covered with live coals Gray says we should have heard that *wench yell* when he started off with the bird

Nov 21st Had Division drill to-day and were out on a large open space of ground where we had plenty of room[18] The last movement we went

[18] "From the 20th to the 28th, division drill of the three brigades and battalion drill, alternately, were the order of the day, General McArthur commanding the

through was a grand charge down a long slope Charged down and many men fell *down* and were *run over* Where we started could be seen thousands of camp fires and a long sweeping view for miles North and South and bounded on the west by a long strip of timber We trod down a large field of cotton just white and ready for the pickers [19]

Nov 22d Weather still fine Had Division drill commencing at 9 o'clock and lasted until noon and the officers took half an hour to go to camp to get their regular bitters Co "G" and "A" were deployed as skirmishers and we charged down the slope and went about one mile and a half on the double quick. Most of us gave out by this time Genl McArthur led a Cavalry charge. He is a fine horseman and rides a beautiful bay horse The General wears a scotch cap or turban which has two little black streamers flying behind McArthur has a pug nose and is a heavy set and hardy looking man and is an Illinois soldier

Nov 23d Sunday: Weather fine and clear Inspection to-day of Division teams and wagons. . . . Harv M Reid refused to go on duty and I sent him to the guard house

I called E P Bye into my tent to-day and told [him] *never* while he was in Co "G" to give me an order as I should never obey him and that I considered him a *sneaking puppy* and that [I] might consider his *hide* worth just about *ten cents* in good currency He protested that he had not wanted the office of Lieut and that he intended to *resign* right away I gave him notice that this was the last I should ever have to say or do with him and

drill of the division personally. This was the first instance of the division being practically instructed in the different movements incident to brigade in line of battle by division. . . . This practical instruction of the troops in movements of every day occurrence, while engaged with the enemy, was heretofore greatly needed, and was of the greatest practical benefit to officers and men." *History of the Fifteenth Regiment, Iowa Veteran Volunteer Infantry . . .* (Keokuk, 1887), 233.

[19] W. L. Watson of the 15th Iowa wrote to the Keokuk *Gate City* on Nov. 21, 1862, describing these maneuvers: "Yesterday our division was out on drill. The 1st and 2d brigades were formed in line of battle in the front, while our brigade, the third, was formed in close column by division in their rear. We changed front and fell in our former position. Skirmishers were then thrown out, and away we went over fences and ditches, through cotton fields and corn fields for some distance, when we again fell back to our former position—the 15th and 16th being ordered in front to charge bayonets. The commands were given, 'Charge bayonets! double quick, march!' Away we went hopping and yelling for about two hundred yards, when we heard the commands, 'Halt! center dress!' The line was soon formed, when the General's aid came up to our Major, telling him the General was highly pleased with the charge, and saying that a better charge never was made." Keokuk *Gate City*, Dec. 3, 1862.

that my opinion of him was just the opinion of the whole Company and knowing the feeling toward himself and how he had obtained the office he was *most welcome* to all he had got thus far. . . .

Nov 25th Cannot get more than 2/3 enough to eat now. The Regulations do not provide for such appetites as we have Had Co drill in forenoon and Bat drill in afternoon Cunningham drilled in latter The Regulations do not *prohibit* him from knowing more than he does

Nov 26th Weather fine. Co on Picket ¾ mile from Camp Drew 5 days Rations Orders are to take the names of all men too sick to travel Rumor says we will march soon About all our tents were taken from us this evening which left some of us out of *doors*

Nov 27th Last night was cold and frosty Eight of us slept under one old tent and with a big log fire at our feet we slept quite well. This morning the Devil entered into (not the swine) Co "A" and most of them being from the "swate emerald Isle" with the help of a half barrel of whiskey managed to give the officers and all the help they could command about all they could do They had been at "Headquarters" on guard and thinking some time in the night that Genl McArthur did not *need* all the whiskey around there they undertook to *convey* a portion to their *natural canteens* but not having it watered as usual it proved too much for them and a *general row* took place Col Belknap ordered a lot of them "bucked and gagged" but that was not done Capt Whitenack finaly got the worst one subdued and they at last succumbed after tearing down their tents and about all their clothes to pieces All the sick and those not able to travel were sent to La Grange to-day . . .

March to Holly Springs Mississippi

Nov 28th In accordance with orders rec'd on Dress Parade last evening we started on the march to-day with 5 days provisions[20] Tie Shepherd, Gray and I gave out about dark We crawled a little off the Road and made a darkey family let us into their cabin We made coffee and laid down on the floor before a big fire place and will sleep here The old

[20] "On November 28th, the organization of all the troops destined for the winter campaign to the rear of Vicksburg being completed, the three corps were put in motion; General Hamilton in command of the left wing, now in front; General McPherson in command of the centre, moving on a parallel road next on the right; and General W. T. Sherman, moving from Memphis southeast toward Abbeville, being the extreme right. The Sixth Division of Hamilton's corps being in the lead of the column, the 3d brigade was in front." *History of the Fifteenth Regiment, Jowa* . . ., 233.

Negro says he belongs on another plantation and is only here to see his wife — says *Mr Van Dorn* is down here a little ways with 300 000 men and *Mr Price* has 150 000 Cavalry We told him to *hush dat talk* and let a poor soldier sleep But just then a nigger baby put in its lip and that was the last we knew

Nov 29th This morning early we arose made coffee, ate breakfast and started on hoping to overtake the Regiment before they got started But we did not find the Regt until night Came on through Holly Springs a beautiful town The people there seemed very *haughty* and in a bad humor Some of the women *spit* at us and made contemptuous faces. But few men could be seen. Cavalry men guarded every street and alley and no man was allowed to disturb anything — not even to go inside a yard to get a drink of water After leaving town we kept south and rapidly gained on the Regt which had started before daylight this morning About 3 oclock we halted and Sargt Gray went into a house to get some fire to make us some coffee and as he came out an officer rode up to us and asked where we belonged and we told him Said he I'll take *care* of you and ordered us to *halt* until a *rear guard* came up While we were halting Gray did some of his *Mexican swearing* Soon the guard came and it had about 50 poor foot sore fellows and were marching them along the road while one rank of guards marched each side of them and one rank in front and one in rear and all the guards with bayonets fixed

The officer ordered us into the pen like cattle and with our heavy load we went for a mile or two The dust was so thick that the guards could not see their file leaders Gray said to me "fix your bayonet" and at the same did so himself — thus we marched about one mile when we being taken for *guards* we gave them the slip and going down close to an old mill off the line of march we kindled a fire and made some coffee and rested Overtook the Regiment about dark and found we had been reported for *promotion* to the *ranks* I took off my shoes and putting my feet in some water soaked my socks loose from my blistered feet There was blisters as large as a silver quarter on the soles of my feet and holding them up by the light I called Capt Hanks attention to them and said If I am reduced to the ranks here is the *cause* If I could have killed one or two men to-night I should have felt compensated and it seems as if nothing but some *fresh blood* would make me rest Gray says if he is reduced he will cut "old Reids' horses tails off to their ears"

Looking for "Dad" Price Van Dorn & Co — Miss

Nov 30th Sunday Feel better this morning but can hardly walk my feet
are so sore The enemy are said to be a few miles ahead and fortified on
the Tallahatchie River Dan Embree Thos Kerr and Wm Campbell and myself had up a small tent but this evening the wind tore it down Last night
it rained about all night. We camped and several regiments went forward
and we could hear heavy cannonading all day to the South [21] Two divisions came up to-day and more are coming from Memphis There must be
at least 50,000 men in this Army Price, Van Dorn and Pemberton are
ahead of us somewhere

Dec 1st This morning was cold and wet and we did not get out early
Have been in camp all day and doing nothing But at sundown order came
to march with three days Rations and before we could get ready the drums
beat and we had to fall in. Some of the wagons were out foraging and we
were hurried greatly News came that the Rebs were retreating from their
forts on the [Tallahatchie] River Our division went ahead with our Brigade
in advance We went on quick and double quick time until we got within
about one mile of the River and marched by the flank into a corn field The
midnight air was damp and cold and we confiscated a lot of dry rails and
made a fire and laid down and tried to sleep

Dec 2d Reveille came this morning about 5 o'clock and we started on
the march at 8 o'clock and went in a South direction Soon came to some
deserted forts and strong earthworks But no enemy. Came on to the Tallahatchie river and halted one hour The Rebs had burned the Bridge and
our men were constructing a temporary one which was very narrow and
bad to drive upon The artillery went over with one horse at a time and
the guns were run over by hand On the North bank of the River was a
heavy redoubt and on the South bank a large fort capable of holding fifteen
guns An abatis was around all and were intended to dispute the crossing

[21] This was probably noise of the skirmishes around Waterford and Lumpkin's
Mills, to the south of Holly Springs, on Nov. 29-30. *Official Records*, Series I, Vol.
XVII, Part I, 465, 491. "Next day, 29th, the march was stopped by the enemy on
the high plateau at Waterford about noon; the 6th division deploying into line of
battle on the north side of the Valley between Waterford and Lumpkin's mill; when
soon after the skirmishers were engaged on both sides, until part of the Federal
cavalry emerged from the timber nearest to the left wing, of the enemy's line; this
at once compelled them to leave the ground. In their haste the enemy left over
300 boxes of tobacco in the place." *History of the Fifteenth Regiment, Iowa . . .*,
233-4.

[of] the Tallahatchie and lacked nothing but the men to defend them The Railroad bridge just above had been burned Going through a wide bottom we came to a succession of hills that were very muddy and steep We soon came to Abbeville a R. R. station Here in the midst of a cold heavy rain we halted and stacked arms and then every man made for the fences to secure wood to make a fire Some went to killing hogs and chickens and ransacking the village for food The musical notes of the porkers could be heard in all directions and the squalling of the feathered inhabitants around every lot Some were holding hogs by the tails and calling for help, and others skinning hogs, and others were hanging up hogs and all around it was a lively scene. Rebs had fired the Depot and it was filled with commissary stores But was too far gone to be saved when we arrived The town has contained say 300 inhabitants and has three or four good houses. Two wells of water and several hundred bushels of sweet potatoes were found and promptly appropriated The country around is woodland and hilly

Van Dorn has had his Headquarters here The Cavalry captured a few prisoners There has been heavy cannonading at the front We went into camp out of the rain under a lot of old stinking beef hides which kept some of the rain from us

Camp near Abbeville Mississippi

Dec 3d This morning the sky was clear and the ground covered with a light frost Found plenty of forage Dan and I found a can of butter for which we paid $1.00 Moved this evening a little over one mile East of Abbeville and in a heavy piece of timber We are close to a fine spring of water We are waiting for supplies and repairing the Railroad

Dec 4th Rained about all day We now have three Sibley tents in the Company and the officers have one Wall tent Have cleaned and leveled off our Camp ground and it looks well . . .

Dec 6th Weather cool clear and beautiful Drew *five* days Rations An order from Genl Hamilton [22] was read on Dress Parade *fining* several men in our and other Regiments for *straggling* on last march The fine is $10.00 apiece and is to be taken out next pay day This will buy some *poor* whiskey for the General and his staff and the poor footsore private will scarcely

---

[22] Brig.-Gen. Charles S. Hamilton, commanded Grant's center in this movement, while Maj.-Gen. James B. McPherson commanded the left, and Maj.-Gen. W. T. Sherman the right wing. Grant, *Personal Memoirs*, 1:423; *Official Records*, Series I, Vol. XVII, Part I, 467.

miss $10.00 from his *extravagant* salary of $13.00 per month   All the troops have gone on from here except our Division

Dec 7th Sunday: Last night was cold and frosty and the ice hung around the edges of the little ponds of water all day   We have built chimneys in our tents and can keep warm   Took a walk down to the mill. An over-shot wheel turns a set of burrs on the little creek and soldiers are running the mill   Our Regt is having a Grist of corn ground   A Patrol guard goes around the camp and arrests all men found rambling around after 9 oclock at night   Gen M. M. Crocker commands Brigade and has his tent just across the creek and in front of our Regiment. Last night Lieut Christofel Co "K" was officer of the guard and he went to his tent after 12 oclock and his men made a good deal of noise   Crocker had the Lieut arrested and several of his men brought before him   He says the 15th Regiment is a set of G-d——d *militia*   He hates our Col Reid like *pisen* and does not speak to him with as much respect as he would to a 1st class government mule   Crocker has several of Co "B" under *guard* close to his head quarters for raising the *devil* with their Capt (Studer)   Studer undertook to *buck* and *gag* a few of the noisest ones but *failed* and they had so much noise about it that Crocker *sent* for them

Dec 8th Weather clear calm and warm enough to go without our coats   The details from our Co are heavy. We have camp guard police fatigue &c   Tom Safford the next worst *wag* to John Cozad — and I made some *hominy* to-day   Gephart Co "D" returned to-day   He is the *first* one to return who was taken prisoner at Shiloh   He reports hard treatment at the hands of the Rebs

Dec 9th Dont know what the weather is outside — but inside of me it has been terrific. Have eat too much corn bread ground at *our mill* consisting of whole grains, cobs &c

Dec 10th Weather fine   There was a detail of 1 Sergt and two men called from our Company to go foraging to-day   I volunteered to go and we went about three miles and found plenty of Corn   Filled ten wagons and Killed 14 hogs   The plantation contained several hundred acres and the owner was in the Southern Army until he died and the widow lives in Abbeville   Qr Master Shannon was along   We also found 37 bales of cotton   There was 25 Negroes on the place and they seemed contented and *happy*   The boys *bought* a lot of stuff from them and paid for it in *facsimile* copies of Confederate money   The copies are manufactured in Phila

and other places and is used here to *purchase* Confederate *produce*[23] This
is the lowest of all *meanness* Better take the property by force than to
impose upon the ignorance of these *poor slaves*

About 200 Confederate prisoners came in to-day from the South. They
were principally Kentuckians and Tennesseans and said that they were *tired*
of the war I am afraid they will get rested and go at it again They report
Price's Army much demoralized and still *skedadling* southward Our Division brought in to-day sixty bales of cotton valued at $32,000

Dec 11th Beautiful warm shining weather There is a general drilling
among all the Regiments Gray says if something new does not come off
soon he will kill a man to start some excitement 850 Rebel prisoners were
brought in from the South to-day They had been captured by our Cavalry
beyond Oxford The rank and file were the hardest looking set I have yet
seen Few of them had Knapsacks and they carried their spare clothes done
up in an old quilt They had no uniforms and were dressed in all colors
and were dirty and filthy Some of them were very footsore and could
hardly walk A six mule team hauled one wagon load of them that had
pegged out The officers were generally well dressed and looked sharp and
obstinate All of them looked haggard and worn out some were in good
spirits and joked along One tall fellow with a big bundle of old clothes
and a *fiddle* said as he walked along, I wonder how long we d——d Rebels
will go before we camp They all when speaking of Genl Price called him
dad

Dec 12th Some rain fell this evening Some few days ago I wrote a letter to Geo W Clark (late of the 3d Iowa) now raising the 34th Ia Regt for
some position in his new Regt and only asked to be transferred in any
capacity whatever and told him how I had been *cheated* here To-day I
received a letter from him and he says that he would like to transfer me
but that an order of the War Dept will not allow the transfer of any enlisted man from one Regt to another. . . .

The Orderly Sergt at Home

Dec 13th . . . The private soldier comes on duty now about every day

[23] The Southerners disliked Federal or "Lincoln" money, and would always take
Confederate bills in preference to more reliable currency. Counterfeit "Rebel"
money was manufactured in the North and sold for $4.00 per 1,000, according to
an advertisement in *Harper's Weekly*, 6:656 (Oct. 11, 1862). See Fred A. Shannon,
The Organization and Administration of the Union Army, 1861–1865 (2 vols., Cleveland, 1928), 1:247.

The corporals about one day in four and the sergents [sic] every ten days except the 1st sergents and they are supposed to be on duty every day and night

The Orderly Sergt of a Co has the most laborious place in it, and only one or two besides myself occupy that position who started out in that position in the 15th Regt The Orderly is the school master and if the *big boys* like him he can teach the school out provided he can stand it to be a *dog* that will run when the Capt and Lieuts *whistle* and is always on hand night and day in sunshine and in storm with his detail at headquarters. The Sergeant Major depends upon him for the delivery of the detail of every kind of guard He must know where every man of his Company sleeps so that he can find [him] day or night without a lantern. He must know at a *glance* without looking at a mans *tongue* whether he is fit for duty. He must keep on a constant lookout to see if every man has the proper clothing. He must know the full accoutrement If a man lacks a cartridge or the least attachment to his gun and that should be a cause of that man *failing* to perform any duty the Capt wants to know of the Orderly why *this is thus* He must make every man come to Roll Call even if he has to stand in mud and snow in his *shirt tail* — he must be made to come to the chalk line No man can be permitted to answer to his name from his bunk or from his eating table — stand up in line and stay there until the last name is called and he has heard the command "break ranks" He must make every complaining man go to the "Surgeons Call" at 8 A. M. and if he can *play off* successfully or is too sick for duty active or graded he is permitted to lay off and the Orderly gets clear of all responsibility for 24 hours

On Sunday morning his duty is to have the men up in good time and *shape* as possible and out in Company *shape* so that when [the] *August* presence of the Capt appears he may feel *proud* of his gallant Company No *stray gray-back* must be seen cantering over the mens clothes as the keen eye of the Capt may *detect* it and then the Orderly will receive a quiet *reprimand* and be told that such things *look* decidedly *unmilitary* Five Roll Calls per day is now our daily allowance

The Orderly must know how much clothing each man has on hand even to a pair of *socks* and he must also see that the men keep themselves washed clean and have no dirt behind their *ears* and that they observe all orders coming from the Regulations, Regimental headquarters or from the Capt Then the Orderly must always help make — or altogether make — out

Muster and Pay Rolls and must know the date of enlistment, time of muster in and the *fate* or *presence* or exact location of each man in the Co, the date of his furlough (if absent) when it expired and must call such man a *deserter* if not back dead or alive at the expiration of leave of absence The Adjutant Genl of Iowa must have a monthly Report of all changes in the Company and the Adjt of the Regt must have his little Morning Report of all present fit for *duty,* sick or absent and thus the *round* goes *round*

Then the Orderly must meet out the most *exact justice* in the matter of *details* from the Co or the men will find fault and some will think they are detailed too often and will whine and complain and he has to stand between the "devil and the deep sea" and set his face like flint against some and others he must humor or punish to keep things balanced The meanest private soldier will *cuss* him if he finds a *maggot* in his bread and the Col will reduce him to the ranks if he should omit the least thing (Not knowing of course that he is *confering* the greatest favor upon the *Victim* of his *rage*) The Commissioned officers of the Co will draw the pay for responsibility and then make the orderly the only responsible man in the Company It would take volumes to tell how much hard and thankless work and duty can be piled on an Orderly Sergt and it would only require a single *Cypher* to tell how few and small the *thanks* he receives for the vigilance watchfulness and care he is compelled to exercise His *lucrative* salary of $20.00 per month is supposed to console him somewhat But $16.00 [*sic* $13.00] per month as a private soldier is full of glory, happiness and contentment compared to the other.

Dec 14th Sunday: Weather cloudy and warm with a southeast wind. Capt Studer officer of the Day *arrested* several men of the *dirty* 16th for washing and committing other nuisances in the little branch out of which we have to use *water* Col Dewey of the 23d Iowa is *dead* Old Whiskey at last laid him *out* as it is laying out many a thousand other men in this Army[24] It is killing more than the Confederates are killing

Dec 15th Have had a terrible storm of rain and wind We have had nothing to eat to-day but *bull beef* and hard tack We have to put one foot on the beef when we pull off a *bite* Had a fire in tent but it almost smoked us out Old "Iron Clad" Cunningham (as the boys called him when he

---

[24] Again Boyd is unjust to the unpopular Dewey who died of erysipelas. A. A. Stuart, *Iowa Colonels and Regiments* . . . (Des Moines, 1865), 382.

bought his bullet proof vest in St Louis) don't seem to be friendly now with Co "G" and more especially with myself. . . .

Dec 16th We have had a cold north wind all day "Iron Clad" fined two men ten dollars each in our Regt and the sentence was read on Dress Parade this eve One man named Tovey of Co "H" was fined $26.00 Dollars (2 months wages) for disobedience of orders . . .

March to Oxford and South — Mississippi

Dec 18th Had orders to be ready to move at 10 o'clock. Marched until 4 Oclock when we crossed a muddy creek 8 miles south of Abbeville and stacked arms and laid down on the ground for the night

Dec 19th Marched at daylight and soon came to Oxford a nice little town and having a College or University General Grants headquarters are here and as our Division filed by each Regt was fronted toward where the General stood on an open porch and close to the street and the men were ordered to give "*three* cheers" for Genl Grant In our Regt only a scattering few cheered But I could hear the men say in a low voice *damn* Genl Grant The Genl bowed and did not seem to care whether we cheered or *cussed* We were taken out of the line of march to see Genl Grant — about one mile None of us would have volunteered to go out of our way 2 rods to see him It seems to be a wonder to *all* why he should be kept in command since the battle of Shiloh The men have no confidence in him [25]

The soldiers occupy all the nice places here and there are many of them surrounded by fine lawns and most beautiful shrubbery and evergreens One large brick building was full of prisoners and they looked out and

[25] This opinion of Grant seemed quite prevalent among the soldiers at this time. Sergeant Onley Andrus of the 95th Illinois wrote of him: "Gen Grant (who by the way is a *Gen* I have but little faith in as a General) made a speech at Grand Junction the other day." Fred Albert Shannon (ed.), *The Civil War Letters of Sergeant Onley Andrus* (Urbana, 1947). *Illinois Studies in the Social Sciences*, Vol. XXVII, No. 4), 28. "Monroe" of the 15th Iowa shared Boyd's opinion: "'U. S.' is a very slow coach, and if he 'can't keep hotel, better ought to take in his sign.'" Keokuk *Gate City*, Oct. 15, 1862. On the other hand, "John" of the 10th Iowa wrote from Oxford, Miss., on Dec. 10, 1862: "Gen. Grant was never more popular with the army than now. As he rides along the lines on review, you can see confidence depicted on every countenance, and his eye sparkes with pride as he looks upon his noble army. And well he may be proud of them—for when the Western soldiers *fight* they *whip.*" Des Moines *Iowa State Register*, Dec. 24, 1862. Grant's universal popularity would come later. In December of 1863, Downing of the 11th Iowa wrote: "General Grant is the man for us yet. All are loud in their praise of Grant, and declare that he is the coming man of the time. . . ." Clark (ed.), *Downing's Civil War Diary*, 157.

passed some jokes   The Negroes are very plenty and stood along the streets by hundreds   Going on south we marched 8 miles and finaly camped on a creek close to a mill   The distance from Abbeville is 19 miles   This place is called Yocona   The country is sand hills with scattering timber

"Dad" Price, Van Dorn & Co Looking for Us — Mississippi

Dec 20th.   Have been busy all day cleaning off our Camp ground and splitting Chestnut timber to drive in the ground to raise our tents on and we have been fixing up as if we were going to winter here   At dark to-night we have up bunks and are very well fixed   Three or four Regiments of Cavalry passed us to-day going *North*   We have discouraging rumors this evening   That the Rebs have run into Holly Springs and have possession of the place — have torn up the Railroad and captured all our *supplies* [26] 9 o'clock PM   Have just received orders to be ready to march at 6 oclock to-morrow morning

On the Retreat Mississippi

Dec 21st Sunday: The Cooks remained up and at work until midnight last night   Cooking *Corn bread*   We use the meal unbolted and we have no sieves   I had to draw Rations for the Co for 4 days   At 4 A M Reveille beat and we divided out the 4 days Rations among the men and were ready at 6 oclock to move   The whole Division commenced moving *Northward* We reached Oxford at 11 oclock   Many of the wom[en] here were visible and wore a look of joy and *triumph* and to indicate that we had got into a *trap* [27]   Great crowds of Negroes stood along the side walks dressed in their best Sunday clothes and many of them looked frightened and dis-

[26] The loss of the supplies at Holly Springs, due to the hit and run raid of Van Dorn, was a blow to Grant's campaign, cutting his long north and south line through the center of Mississippi, and forcing a retreat north. Holly Springs had been left under the command of Colonel Robert C. Murphy of the 8th Wisconsin. Grant wrote of this disaster: "The capture was a disgraceful one to the officer commanding but not to the troops under him. . . . Murphy was . . . warned of Van Dorn's approach, but made no preparations to meet him. He did not even notify his command." Grant, *Personal Memoirs*, 1:432, 433. On January 3, 1863, Murphy was "dismissed from the service of the United States, to take effect from the 20th day of December, 1862, the date of his cowardly and disgraceful conduct." *Official Records*, Series I, Vol. XVII, Part I, 516.

[27] "The news of the capture of Holly Springs and the destruction of our supplies caused much rejoicing among the people remaining in Oxford. They came with broad smiles on their faces, indicating intense joy, to ask what I was going to do now without anything for my soldiers to eat." Grant, *Personal Memoirs*, 1:435. When Grant advised them that he intended to live off the country, the smiles soon turned to dismay.

heartened that we were going *back* Here we met Genl Quimby's Division coming in on another road Halted at the Creek where we had formerly camped and ate dinner At Sundown we were in our old camp near Abbeville having marched 19 miles to-day Weary and worn out we slept on our old bunks once more

Camp at Holly Springs Mississippi

Dec 22d Weather warm and *roads good* Started at day break toward Holly Springs Had Knapsacks guns and 40 rounds and traveled very fast At noon we ate dinner at the Tallahatchie on our old camp ground. Made a hard march until 7 P M After dark we entered Holly Springs and went through the town and halted on the North side Soon as the men could get their things off they commenced going for things generaly. Every one was gone except those who could not travel from fatigue As for myself I was so far gone that I could not get up to move I could hear hogs squeal and chickens squall in all directions By 11 oclock we had devoured some fresh pig Sergt Gray had secured for our mess a fine Pig. He can hear a hog grunt or a chicken breathe as far as any other man in this Army . . .

Dec 23d Reveille at 4 A. M. The men were very tired and sore but with about the average amount of groaning and *swearing* they got out. At 8 A M we were told that we should not march to-day The wagons were unloaded and foraging parties sent out [28] Almost all the men left Camp and were soon scattered all over the town in a few hours Soldiers could be seen everywhere Out of the cellar of a large brick residence close to our camp there came a constant stream of men and others kept going in and it resembled a *hive of bees* I went over and found the molasses running about 2 inches deep on the floor of the cellar and the men were wading through and carrying off various articles The occupants of the house were inside and locked up and no one outside except a little Negro boy Around were all the indications of Wealth Beautiful shrubbery and trees and vines and flowers and arbors While I was looking around I heard a *row* inside and soon seen a soldier come through the kitchen window heels first and a boot close to his *rear* and attached to a pair of *shoulder straps* About this time I had *business* toward camp

[28] "I was amazed at the quantity of supplies the country afforded. It showed that we could have subsisted off the country for two months instead of two weeks without going beyond the limits designated. This taught me a lesson which was taken advantage of later in the campaign when our army lived twenty days with the issue of only five days' rations by the commissary." *Ibid.*, 435.

Going down to the "Clayton House" a large frame building I noticed a great crowd around the front door with their arms full of books and papers. I came around the house and just then a lady raised the window and called to me and asked me if I was an officer I replied that I was not a commissioned officer Said she for Gods sake keep the "soldiers from breaking into my room they have possession of the house and I fear they will *Kill me*" I told her not to fear as no man would disturb her. She was a rather good looking woman and had four little children with her This evening this *same* woman was arrested for *shooting* one of our men who was on guard at the "Clayton House" (2 days ago) She cowardly shot him although he was guarding her property This whole town was literly gutted to-day[29]

Van Dorn was here two days ago with a large force of Cavalry and surprised what few men we had here Then the Rebs blew up several buildings right in the Centre of the town and burned the Depots and all the rolling stock and Warehouses and destroyed more than one million Dollars worth of our supplies and also captured several of our Pay Masters with large amounts of Money.[30] Long trains of cars were burned with all their contents and nothing but the irons and trucks stand on the track for almost a *mile* There has been a fearful destruction of property and many of the citizens were killed by the explosions The 101st Ills Infty and the 2d Ills Cavalry had been left to guard the Post The Cav fought as long as they could and then had to *retreat* The Infantry *surrendered* at the first summons and scarcely fired a gun Col Murphy of the 8th Wisconsin commanded

I found the Court House square filled with horses, cannon and ammunition Women with band-boxes and other traps were leaving in all directions The soldiers were in every house and garret and cellar, store and church, and nook and corner. The streets were white with all kinds of paper and men were running with their arms full of books and ledgers and

[29] Sergeant Downing, of the 11th Iowa, was in Holly Springs that day. "The rebels before leaving town burned several houses, altogether some two or three squares, besides burning about one million of our rations, and we are again short of food. On that account the boys are not in the best of humor, and every man has practically a free hand to take anything that he can use or that he may want; and there are no officers out looking for corporals to reduce to the ranks as was done on our way south." Clark (ed.), *Downing's Civil War Diary*, 88-9.

[30] Grant reported $400,000 worth of property taken; Van Dorn claimed $1,500,000. *Official Records*, Series I, Vol. XVII, Part I, 478, 503.

one lot of soldiers had their arms full of Confederate *bank notes* which were perfect in all except the Presidents signature (I think the President did not have time to sign) The boys said they could do that *themselves* On the east side of the square the large brick buildings which we saw there two weeks ago were now one vast shapeless mass of ruins Some of these buildings had been stored with shell and other ammunition and explosive Material Fully one half the fine buildings on North side of the square were likewise blown to pieces

There had been a Bank in one of them and some gold and silver had been melted among the rubbish and the soldiers were in digging to their knees in the brick bats Sudden and complete destruction has overtaken this city When we went down through here the women and even the children could insult us in every way and we did not disturb a hair of their heads But it remained for their *own friends* to complete their woe If the Confederates treat their own people thus what would they do with their enemies I came to Genl Grants headquarters and saw him talking to an Officer He stood with his hands in his pockets like a common farmer and looked as unconcerned as if he was selling eggs at 2 cts per dozen Everyone thinks Grant has made another big blunder in allowing the Army thus to be cut off from our base of supplies The Col Murphy who surrendered here is the same man who surrendered about 100,000 000$ [*sic*] worth of supplies at Iuka to Price He is called a *traitor*

I came by a fine large Roman Catholic Church A lot of soldiers were in the building some were taking the organ to pieces and had the pipes out blowing on them and throwing them away Up in the pulpit was a squad playing *cards* and another lot were scattering the library over the floor One daring and reckless soldier climbed to the pinnacle of the temple and took off the little silver image of "Jesus" that stood there. It was at a giddy height but he got it — said to be worth several hundred dollars Every portion of the *fated city* seemed given over to *pillage* and destruction and no hand was raised to save anything from the general *sack and ruin*

Finely dressed ladies were leaving on all the streets and going God knows where Women and children were standing in their houses wailing with the most piteous cries Young girls whose eyes were red with weeping peered from behind the curtains of the windows and gazed listlessly upon the passing throngs that crowded the streets No insults were offered any women or citizen that I saw or heard of

When I had witnessed all this destruction and terror my heart almost ceased to beat when I thought of the sadness and woe that is caused by this inhuman war of brother against brother and how the innocent shall suffer in the cause of treason and Rebellion

Railroad communication is completely broken up and we are about out of provisions and Memphis [is] now our base of supplies which is a long way off   Marion Mart one of our Co left here was taken prisoner and parolled by the enemy

Dec 24th   From poverty and want we have suddenly become rich and *stuck* up. We have been sleeping on slanting rails and on the cold frosty earth or under a mule wagon or indeed we have slept in all kinds of places with a stone for a pillow   But we are above that now   We have mahogany bedsteads and the finest lounges that this Market affords   The tents are not large enough to hold all the fine furniture now on hands. Dan Embree, Gray, Harv Reid and I are all in one tent   We have fine Carpet down, a stove and more stuff than we actually *need*. We are short of provisions but shall *trust* to Gray [31]

Dec 25th Christmas   We are not so *merry* as we might be. No demonstration in Camp would indicate this Holiday   Have nothing to eat but a little Corn bread and some tough beef   Genl Logans Division went North to-day

Dec 26th   To-day has been wet and gloomy and has rained about all day. A great train of wagons left here for Memphis to bring provisions   A heavy guard went along and also took about 1000 prisoners or parolled men left here by the enemy — but will have to be exchanged before they can bear arms again   The 101st Ills was also taken and had to run the gauntlet of abuse as they marched by   That Regt will be *notoriously* known hereafter

Dec 27th . . .   Gray and I went up town this evening and after rambling around for some time when a man with "birds" on his shoulders (a Colonel) ordered every man *arrested* who had no Pass signed by Division

---

[31] Downing wrote on Dec. 25: "We are still on half rations. But in spite of it, the boys are all enjoying themselves. They are taking everything that they can lay their hands on, carrying to their tents couches, rockers, chairs, tables, books, bric-a-brac—in fact, all kinds of household articles. Some of the boys, who are lovers of fancy books, sent home by express some of the most costly bound volumes. Holly Springs has certainly paid dear for burning our supplies." Clark (ed.), *Downing's Civil War Diary*, 89.

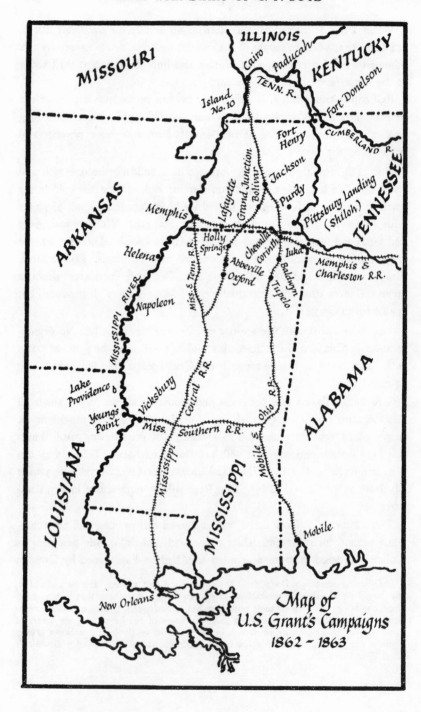

Map of
U.S. Grant's Campaigns
1862 ~ 1863

Commander — and set him to *work*. Gray and I had pressing business at Camp as we had no Passes. "We done left" We are living hard now. Out of coffee and to-day we drew 6 days [rations] Consisting of *Corn meal*, 1 Box ckrs 2 shoulders of Meat and some wheat for coffee No article can take the place of Coffee to the soldier He carries it in a little sack in his pocket and watches it as he does his scanty pay of $13.00 per mo When the weather is cold and wet and he is deprived of this favorite beverage he becomes revolutionary and almost unmanageable With his daily allowance he will bear and forbear — but without it he may *rebel* at any moment

Dec 28th *Sunday*: Had Inspection at 10 AM Gray and Dan Embree went out and found a fat hog and a few turnips and we shall live while we live . . .

On the march toward Memphis
Lafayette sta Tennessee

Dec 30th Have traveled 18 miles to-day in the direction of Memphis It rained some this forenoon and the roads are bad We are camped tonight close to a branch of Wolf River and have plenty of good dry rails to burn

Dec 31st We were *rear guard* to-day and had a hard time Came 18 miles and carried our Knapsacks and all our traps Tonight we are camped close to Lafayette a station on the M & C R R [32] When we stacked arms to-night some went for Water and some went for wood and some went for *hog* In a little while the timber around camp was laden with *skinned* hogs, cattle &c

Last night was cold and frosty and this morning the ground was frozen Our gun barrels felt very cold to our bare hands. This winds up 1862 with its joys and a multitude of sorrows We are now in the dense dark wilderness of uncertainty and the silver lining of the dark cloud of war is not visible How long shall this struggle last no one seems to know but *He* who knowest all things.

[32] The Memphis & Charleston Railroad. Lafayette Station, on the railroad, was just across the northern border of Mississippi, in Tennessee. This northward movement of the troops was in preparation for the removal of Grant's headquarters from central Mississippi to Memphis. Grant, *Personal Memoirs*, 1:438.

PART IV

LAFAYETTE TO LAKE PROVIDENCE, LOUISIANA

January 1, 1863 to March 14, 1863

The Canal at Lake Providence

Camp at Lafayette Jennessee

Jany 1st 1863 Companies "G" and "D" were ordered to Lafayette station to guard the commissary stores just come in from Memphis[1] We relieved the 93d Indiana We have established a few forts around the depot and water tank Lafayette has but one citizen left and that is a widow woman. The town has had about 150 inhabitants There is but one good dwelling in the place There is a fine large brick depot and warehouse Our Surgeon took the best house in town for his headquarters But had hardly got it warmed before Hugh T Reid came and dispossessed him and proceeded to fix himself in it. But he had scarcely become used to its comforts when Genl Quinby [Brig.-Gen. Isaac F. Quinby, 13th Army Corps] came along and notified Mr Reid that he should want that "house" for his own use So Mr Reid took an humble abode and "grated" his teeth Guerrillas swarm all through this country and last night one of the 93d Indiana was wounded on Picket We cannot forage here without a guard

We found a few copies of the "Chicago Times" here. It is the best Rebel authority to be had and it says Burnside lost 12,500 men in the late battle[2]

---

[1] The 15th Iowa, as part of the 3rd — Crocker's — Brigade of the 6th Division of the 17th Army Corps, was assigned to the protection of the Memphis & Charleston RR. Stationed at Lafayette, Tenn., the Regiment took part in several skirmishes against Rebel guerrillas. [William W. Belknap], *History of the Fifteenth Regiment, Iowa Veteran Volunteer Infantry* . . . (Keokuk, 1887), 236.

[2] The Chicago *Times* was a Democratic newspaper which grew increasingly bitter against Lincoln as the war progressed. Wood Gray, *The Hidden Civil War: The Story of the Copperheads* (New York, 1942), 98-9. The battle referred to is probably Burnside's heavy loss of 12,000 Union troops at the Battle of Fredericksburg on December 13, 1862. T. Harry Williams, *Lincoln and His Generals* (New York, 1952), 199.

We have received no Mail since we left Abbeville. All think the mails have been cut off because of the bad news. The weather is cool and fine

Jany 2d The great train of wagons from Memphis commenced unloading at the Depot and Warehouse last night. There was so much noise no one could sleep The men detailed to unload the wagons had their regular rations of whiskey every two hours and some of them got a little too loose before morning The[y] bursted open barrels and boxes all over the platform and tore things up generaly The teamsters were about all *tight* and several of them let their teams run away and such halooing and shouting and swearing I never heard

An Engine came up from Moscow and found the track clear to this point Genl McArthur was on the Engine. Soon some cars came down with a lot of Engineers and workmen They run west to repair a bridge about two miles But just as they got to work about 20 guerrillas attacked them The guard a Company of Wis troops all ran back here without making a fight Instantly there was an alarm and the "long roll" beat and we fell into line The 13th [Iowa] with our Regt [3] was hurried northward and gone about half a day. We captured 75 head of hogs and 30 head cattle that would *not* take the oath of allegiance to the United States

A train of cars left this afternoon for Corinth loaded with provisions To-day 2 guerrillas were captured and brought in. One of them had 40 Negroes hid out and they too came in and went into a little frame house. Such a lot of pagans I never saw They are almost naked and as ignorant as beasts from old grand mother down to suckling child Their Master had them hid out with a lot of mules horses and hogs and our men *drove* them all in *together* The aristocracy goes with the field hands "The tail goes with the hide" in this new order of things

This eve our boys being on guard at the Depot discovered a barrel of white sugar among a lot of barrels of salt and they rolled it under the Depot and after dark brought it to camp and we shall have syrup and *taffy* for some time

Jany 3d Last night was a terrific one The wind which had been blewing [*sic*] so hard all day increased to a hurricane and blue [*sic*] with fury all night tearing down tents and everything loose About 2 oclock at night a heavy rain storm set in which added much to our uncomfortable condition

---

[3] According to Belknap's account, it was the 15th and 16th Iowa Regiments which took part in this foray. [Belknap], *History of the Fifteenth Iowa . . .*, 236.

In the darkness could be heard men driving stakes and hallooing to everybody and swearing like the "Army in Flanders" This morning the water
stood about one inch in our tent Most of our Company were at the Depot
and their tents were blown down and everything wet, and when they were
relieved came to camp and had a good time raising tents Corp Kitchell
cooks for our mess and we have plenty to eat and are *happy*

An order came from Genl Grant to have our arms in good condition and
to be ready for *action* at a moments notice Van Dorn threatens our com-
munications again and may strike us at any time

Jany 4th Sunday: Last night the rain pounded down most of the night
But this morning the sky was clear except a heavy bank of clouds to the
eastward The sun has dried up the mud Cars are running from Memphis
to Corinth. We get no mail. It is suppressed or destroyed News of fighting at Vicksburgh and Murphreysboro. . .[4]

Jany 5th Lieut Fisk came to us to-day How glad we were to see him
Nine months ago he was captured at Pittsburgh Landing and he has been a
prisoner in Montgomery, Macon, Selma and other places in the South He
looks well and his fine new suit in great contrast with our weather beaten
uniforms The Lieut brought me $5.00 and 68 postage stamps for which I
was very grateful

Have been very busy all day on Pay Rolls — Had an alarm in Camp and
were just *two* minutes getting into line with our arms Went Northward
two miles and met some of our cavalry who told us there was no enemy in
that direction and we returned The night was cold and frosty

Jany 7th To-day has been wet muddy and gloomy. No mail and no
news This eve Elias Reid and David Elliott returned from leave of absence

[4] This "news of fighting" probably refers to Sherman's failure to reach Vicksburg
from the Yazoo River, which flows into the Mississippi above Vicksburg. Sherman,
in conjunction with Admiral Porter, had transported 30,000 men from Memphis down
the Mississippi to the Yazoo and up that river to Chickasaw Bayou, reaching there
on December 26, 1862. They expected to be supported by Grant at the rear of
Vicksburg, not knowing of Grant's setback at Holly Springs. The swampy terrain
between the Yazoo and Vicksburg, coupled with large forces within that city, forced
Sherman to withdraw after heavy losses. *Memoirs of Gen. W. T. Sherman . . .* (2
vols., New York, 1891), 1:317–21. The Battle of Murfreesboro (or Stone River) in
eastern Tennessee was an encounter between Bragg and Rosecrans, who had replaced Buell in command of the Army of the Cumberland, in which the Union
forces had been successful. The bitterly fought battle had lasted from December 31,
1862, to January 4, 1863. *Personal Memoirs of P. H. Sheridan . . .* (2 vols., New
York, 1888), 1:237–45; Otto Eisenschiml and Ralph Newman, *The American Iliad . . .*
(Indianapolis, 1947), 291–314.

Both were wounded at Corinth Samuel Roberts who was taken prisoner at the same time also came in and looking well Sam Stanford [Stanfield] returned from *desertion* He deserted July 13th and escaped into Ills where he was arrested and taken to St Louis He is a big strong fellow and looks rather *sheepish*

Jany 8th Our mess has been busy putting on an addition to our tent of lumber and now we are very comfortable We have a stove inside But alas for all the comfort a soldier can hope for or dream of. Just at dark an order came to be ready at a moments notice to *march*

Uncle John Steele of the 4th Ills Cav. came over and we had a long talk This forenoon while we were building our *hut* we ran out of nails and Corp Kitchell and I went down town to find some and seeing a paling fence we knocked off a few palings and carried them to camp for the nails and the wood. About the time we got to the tent Col Reid rode up and enquired for the men who had taken the palings We told him that we were the *lads* He said when he wanted the town *torn down* and the fence taken away from around his horses he would send for *us* He ordered us to take the palings back and nail them on where we found them We told him it should be done and with our loads on our shoulders we *countermarched*

Jany 9th There was four nails in each paling and we pulled *three* out and tacked the other nail on just enough to hold till morning and then we packed about one half the palings back and hid them The bal of the company thought it a good joke on us — but we thought our *generous* commander had not made much out of the *operation*

Jany 10th Weather clear and warm Drew *five* days Rations Two trains from Memphis to-day Bad news from Vicksburgh Genl Sherman made an assault on the place and we have lost heavily and the Army has fallen back on the Yazoo and are mostly at Napoleon Ark Banks and Farragut failed to come up the River and the whole plan failed [5]

Jany 11th Sunday: Clear and fine weather I have made out three Pay Rolls today I do not make it my choice of working to-day but military necessity compels

March toward Memphis Tennessee

Jany 12th This morning at 7 o'clock A M Brigade started with our Regt in advance The day was fine and we traveled steadily Came through

[5] This would indicate that they had received confirmation of the fighting referred to in footnote 4.

Collierville a small village entirely deserted   The 17th Iowa was here   Saw Lieut Woodrow   He has resigned   16 miles from Lafayette we passed through Germantown a place of about 400 inhabitants   We came on westward 4 miles and camped close to a sta[tion] on the Railroad.   Came 22 miles to-day and many of the men gave out   Lieut Fisk was very *sore footed* . . .

Camp at *Memphis*

Jany 13th   We started at daylight this morning and made a march of 9 miles and came to the suburbs of Memphis   Here we were brought into line and notified to sign Pay Rolls   We put up our tents and signed Rolls — then I took a ramble thro' Memphis   It was 2 miles to the River from camp   Saw a camp of Contrabands containing old and young 1500 and they were packed into a building about 200 x 150 feet   They were a mass of filthy and abandoned creatures   Down at the wharf there was a long line of steamers lying along the bank   Saw one gun boat anchored in the stream   There is a view up the River of about five miles and ten or twelve miles down the stream   Memphis is situated on high bluffs and has a beautiful location   The business portion is built of brick   Lafayette Square is the center of the city and is a beautiful Park full of Evergreens and tame squirrels are numerous among the trees and follow strangers all around

Whiskey O Whiskey!   Drunk men staggered on all the streets   In every store   The saloons were full of *drunk men*   The men who had fought their way from Donelson to Corinth and who had met no enemy able to whip them now surrendered to Genl *Intoxication* [6]   Some were on the side walks and both hands full of brick bats and swearing that the side walks were made for soldiers and not for any d——d niggers   Some were wallowing in the streets dead drunk others were being loaded on drays and into wagons and tied hand and foot and taken to the Calabose or guardhouse or to Camp   Several of Co "G" are down this evening with the general complaint   The whiskey here seems to be very effective at short range

I found some wheat bread the first I have seen for two months   Sergt Gray came near getting shot this evening about dark   He was *full* and in camp   He saw a mounted orderly coming past in hot haste and he halted

---

[6] Excessive drinking remained a problem throughout the war. "Since drinking was largely a matter of opportunity, intemperance was most common during changes of station, especially those requiring passage through cities, on holidays and at paytime." Bell I. Wiley, *The Life of Billy Yank* . . . (Indianapolis, 1951), 253.

him and made the orderly give him the countersign Afterwards the aide
discovered that he had been delayed without cause and he drew his revolver and if Gray had not run and hid himself he would have got a bullet
Gray gave him the dodge around the tents and finaly reached one where he
lay down and the boys covered him up and he was snoring away in 2 seconds

Jany 14th This has been a most disagreeable day. The rain poured down
and our tents leaked and we have no wood nor stoves Many men lay in
the *gutter* or the guard house last night Some of Co "K" came over to our
tent this eve and bored us for a long time They were *drunk* and came over
to tell me that I was the best Orderly in the Regt and the most abused man
— I humored them some and finaly got them to leave Anything almost is
better than the sympathy of a *drunk* man About two thirds of the Regiment went down into the city and not more than one third returned The
spree still goes on

Jany 15th This morning when we awoke the snow was pouring down
and the camp and the ground was covered to the depth of ten inches of
solid snow right here in the City of Memphis in the state of Tennessee and
in the midst of the *hot* southern Confederacy We call this very *cool* treatment We had heretofore been received in the *warmest* manner of which
the natives were capable Very few remained in camp to get breakfast

The camp guards stuck their bayonets into the ground — left their beats
and slunk away to some house Sergt Gray was equal to this occasion as
he has been to all others and he was soon out. When he came back he told
us he had made up his mind to *reside* in a two story frame house in the city
and had made arrangements for *meals* &c We followed him and found
good quarters in a large frame building The men came here many of them
barefooted and their clothes in rags and they have been buying and *stealing*
a great deal of stuff to-day. A Company will go into a store to fit themselves
out in boots and before they get away about one half will have bought
boots and the other half stolen about the same amount of stuff I attended
the Theatre this eve The house was full of soldiers and about one half of
them were *full* and there was a jolly time and no mistake The play was the
"Hidden Hand" and was very good

Jany 16th The weather is milder and the snow thawed some The men
are scattered all over the city and laying around loose One week here will
be worse for them than six months in the field

Jany 17th The snow thawed considerable to-day The 34th Iowa came from below to-day I went down to the River to see them I found them on two steamers guarding 4800 Confederate prisoners captured at Arkansas Post [7] The 34th is in bad spirits about nine tenths of the men are sick and such a discouraged and disheartened lot of men I never saw The 15th Regt in her *gloomiest* days did not look so bad. Col Clark looked well but the men from exposure and the *smallpox* looked awful

The Cabins of the two vessels were packed with sick and dying men They lay in their filth so close that it was difficult to walk thro the boat [8] The prisoners were the best looking set of men that I have seen in the Confederate service The Rebel Genl Churchill and 300 Confederate officers were at one end of a boat in the Cabin [9] Their friends here in Memphis came down by hundreds and brought them many things Nothing seemed to *comfort* them like copies of the "Chicago Times" They devoured their contents with more relish than their food Most of them were Texas and Ark men. To night is piercing cold and we can hardly keep warm with all the lumber and palings we can get into the big fire place Gray is too *full for utterance* tonight This afternoon he went to the Capt and told him he

[7] The 34th Iowa, to which Boyd later transferred as a lieutenant, had been mustered into service at Burlington, Oct. 15, 1862, and had fought with Sherman at Chickasaw Bayou and at Arkansas Post, a fort on the Arkansas River, about forty miles from its confluence with the Mississippi River. Arkansas Post had been captured by Sherman and McClernand in an expedition undertaken in conjunction with Admiral David D. Porter on January 11, 1863. The fall of the Fort there — known as Fort Hindman — was of great aid to the Union forces in protecting their assault on Vicksburg. See Sherman, *Memoirs*, 1:324–31; *Personal Memoirs of U. S. Grant* (2 vols., New York, 1885), 1:439-40; Admiral David D. Porter, *The Naval History of the Civil War* (New York, 1886), 289–93; *The War of the Rebellion . . . Official Records . . .* (Washington, 1886), Series I, Vol. XVII, Part I, 698–796 (hereafter referred to as *Official Records*); [J. S. Clark], *The Thirty-fourth Iowa Regiment . . .* (Des Moines, 1892), 7–10.

[8] "One hesitates to attempt a description of the suffering of this trip to Chicago which resulted from packing and jamming of about 5,500 men on three moderate sized boats. The cases of small pox were greatly multiplied in the regiment and before we reached St. Louis the disease broke out among the prisoners. . . . The state rooms were filled with sick. The floors of the cabin were covered with the sick of our own regiment, and also sick rebels, all lying closely together, some with fever, some with pneumonia, some with measles, some with small pox, all with chronic diarrhea. There were not enough well men to properly guard the prisoners and care for the sick." [Clark], *Thirty-fourth Iowa Regiment . . .*, 11.

[9] "Among the 4,791 prisoners were Gen. [Thomas J.] Churchill, rebel general commanding, and his staff; seven colonels; about fifteen lieutenant-colonels and majors, and 330 other officers." *Ibid.*, 10.

had concluded to *resign* and turned over his gun and accoutrements to him
He supposes that he can *resign* as he has got his whiskey *mixed*

Big Spree at Memphis Tennessee

Jan 18th Sunday: This morning at 8 oclock we struck tents and marched
to the Landing and when we got to the bluff above we formed in line and
had to stand in the slush and mud until 4 oclock in the evening when we
got aboard the Steamer Minnehaha that same old boat that carried us to
Pittsburgh Landing [10] We have a superstitious idea about this vessel and
that she will again carry us into some *trouble* Our Regt and the 16th Iowa
are both crowded onto this boat Co "G" is located on the boiler deck and
here we and Co "B" and the entire baggage of the Regiment are all packed
The place is as dark as Hades We cannot see in the day time without
candles The men climbed on top of the baggage and some into the bunks
of the crew and wherever else they could until every space a foot square
was filled

During the night — while still at the wharf — the men run the *guards*
and made a raid on a large lot of Sutlers goods on shore They carried on
board all kinds of goods — especialy cases of canned fruit and champagne
and whiskey with wine and brandy Hats, caps, boots and shoes Soon
all this became badly *mixed* and the roar commenced. Such a bedlam was
never seen The men were soon *drunk* and the whole command became
demoralized — The most of the officers were of course in the Cabin but
their slumbers were soon disturbed by the *earthquake* around the boiler
deck and they came down and tried to quiet the *different drinks* that had
been taken but it was no use they could do nothing with them The men
swore they were going to *Vicksburgh* and to *hell* and they intended to have
a *good time now* One fellow fell overboard and was *fished* out and laid
out in the Cabin to *dry* Co "A" were almost all *drunk* and were fighting
like dogs among themselves all night and several badly used noses were
visible in the flickering candlelight

Sobering up at Memphis Tennessee

Jany 19th Last night there was a tremendous rain which drove the men
from the hurricane deck and they came down and huddled about the boilers

[10] "January 18th the 15th and 16th Iowa were embarked on the steamer Minnehaha . . . and the several regiments and batteries of the 6th division were embarked on fourteen other steamers, the Platte Valley being the flagship. On the
20th the 6th division had 6,115 men present and 16 pieces of artillery. On this day

I never saw so many *noses* out of repair and mutilated faces and black eyes as there are aboard this boat Drinking and fighting filled up last nights hours.

To-day was cool and cloudy and a light fog hung over the river The men run rampant over the boat some were fighting and some were *hugging* each other and some were patching up their wounds and some hung their heads over the boat and cast up their accounts To be shut up among such a gang of *brutes* makes me think that I should just as soon be in *hell* at once

Major Cunningham Capt Mattesen [Madison] and Capt Studer received their *Release* from the service here and will leave for more *congenial* places Cunningham never came to bid Co "G" *good-bye* but he *sneaked* away and was only too glad to escape without seeing any of us. He is one of those noiseless *vipers* that lie in the sunshine and when no warning can be given his victim he will strike at him when defenseless I shall never forget how popular he was when elected Captain of Co "G" Nor shall I forget how mean he has treated the Company and with what *little regret* we feel at his timely departure He carries away with him his *"bullet proof vest"* and over $30.00 of commutation money that belongs to the poor sick men who are now alive and the joint property of some who have gone to *premature graves* for the want of some little delicacy or necessity that might have kept them *alive* While he remained he was one of the *vermin* that lived around the kennel of H. T. Reid and through that meanest of all men he inherited all the Rank he received above Capt

Capt Mattison was liked by his men and Capt Studer was a good fellow but he could not *adjust* himself to the men of Co "B" whom he called *"Arabs"* Capt Hedrick of Co "K" will take Cunninghams place as Major of the Regiment and as good a whole souled man as ever carried a sword

A Few Thoughts at Memphis Tenn

Great opposition is being made some places in the North to President Lincolns Proclamation of Emancipation and the states of Indiana and Illinois seem bent upon fixing up a *rotten* Peace with the Southern Confederacy The times look gloomy and the darkness that surrounds the Republic can almost be *felt* *Traitors* at home and defeat in the field seem to be working

the fleet started toward Vicksburg, where several corps were already stationed on the Louisiana side of the river, now to try unitedly the solution of the great military problem which had just proved a failure to the winter expedition on land, and also at Chickasaw Bayou." [Belknap], *History of the Fifteenth Iowa* . . ., 238-9.

a Counter Revolution I am satisfied more every day that many of our leading men care for nothing beyond their salaries and what they can steal
Treason is gnawing at our vitals at home and men in the army are discouraged

Shall I ever *forget* how dark and *intensely hopeless* every *feature* of our
struggle *looks now* The eastern army is totaly routed and the enemy is
strong and defiant *everywhere* There are almost enough traitors at home to
wipe out the loyal men who are not in the army Hired [illegible] and
assassins are being sent to Canada to burn our cities along the Lakes and
assassinate our Rulers — through their agents and sympathizers in the
United States Men in our ranks are getting letters from "Copperheads"
in the North advising them to *desert* the *abolition* army This may be that
dark hour just before dawn. I know it cannot get much darker [11]

Embarkation of Grant's Army at Memphis, Tenn

Jany 20th Just at noon the steamers of the fleet got up steam and in half
an hour the flag-ship "Platte Valley" backed into the stream and turned
her bow to the *North* The other vessels followed and when above the City
a mile or two the Platte turned in a *counter march* and the other vessels
followed amid the music of the bands on board each vessel and the firing
of cannon on shore Thousands stood on the shore and waved flags and
cheered as the long winding fleet turned to the South All the boats were
loaded with the blue uniforms of the great Army which had never yet been
defeated together with the waving flags and shouts of the men whose faces
were set for the Western Gibraltar of the Confederacy at Vicksburgh It
was the most *inspiring* sight yet seen on the old "father of waters" on this
January morning of the New Year This was the great *advance* and every
one seemed hopeful as we turned toward the South

We went in the following order [12]

[11] This was indeed a "period of despair" in the North and among the Union
forces. Losses in the field, both on the Potomac and the Mississippi, and the increased activities of the "Peace Democrats" — the so-called Copperheads — who
pled for a peace without victory were pressing hard on Lincoln and the administration. For the newest work on the Copperhead movement, see Gray, *The Hidden
Civil War* . . ., especially Chapter VI which covers the period from December 13,
1862, to the fall of Vicksburg on July 4, 1863, a victory which — together with that
at Gettysburg — marked the resurgence of confidence in the Union Army and
among the Northern Unionists.

[12] Although Boyd lists 12 boats, with names for eleven, most accounts give any-
where from 13 to 15 as the number in this fleet. [Belknap], *History of the Fifteenth*

1st Platte Valley	7th Gate City
2d Jennie Deans	8th (Blank)
3d Marie Deming	9th Arago
4th Dilligent	10th Superior
5th Sunnyside	11th Madison City
6th Minnehaha	12th St Louis

These vessels kept at a distance of 200 to 400 yards apart as we glided down the stream During the afternoon we did not see much except the wide waste of waters — for the River is high and occasionally a *sad looking plantation* on the Arkansas shore Once in awhile we could see a hole in the woods with a cabin and a few small fields At dark the fleet drew in toward the Arkansas shore behind a dense forest — and a few men went ashore to cook. Here we shall remain all night.

Memphis to Vicksburgh, Mississippi River

Jany 21st We sailed at daylight and by 11 oclock we were at Helena Ark and stayed there *two* hours The 33d 40th and 26th Iowa Regts were there Also the 3d and 4th Cavalry and such shouting and cheering and shaking of hands I never saw The guards could not keep the men on the boats. I saw no one I knew Helena is a town of about 1000 inhabitants in ordinary times but now contains more "yanks" than natives The town lies on both level and high ground Back of the place are steep and rugged hills almost naked of timber while next to the River the ground is level and wet It is fortified by a strong work near the centre of the town and by fortifications above and below

Leaving Helena we kept on down the stream and followed the current

Iowa . . ., 238, gives 14 led by the Platte Valley; 15 is the number given by Lurton Dunham Ingersoll, *Iowa and the Rebellion* . . . (Philadelphia, 1866), 254; "C. E." wrote to the Muscatine *Weekly Journal* on Jan. 28, 1863, that the troops embarked on "thirteen transports"; his letter was published in the Feb. 6, 1863, issue. On Grant's orders, transports for 16,000 men were ordered to Memphis; an order which practically cleared the Mississippi and Ohio of boats except between Memphis and Vicksburg. *Official Records*, Series I, Vol. XVII, Part I, 556. See also Grant, *Personal Memoirs*, 1:441-2. When the fleet reached Milliken's Bend, nearly opposite Vicksburg, more than 100 steamboats had gathered there, bringing Union troops south to the siege of Vicksburg. [Belknap], *History of the Fifteenth Iowa* . . ., 239. This was the beginning of the great move upon Vicksburg via the Mississippi. Grant had failed in his planned double-pronged attacks — Sherman from the Yazoo and Grant from the rear of Vicksburg. McClernand, who had for a time been given command of the Mississippi attack by Lincoln, and who had gone with Sherman to Arkansas Post on what Grant had at one time termed a "wild-goose chase," was now definitely subordinated to Grant in command. *Official Records*, Series I, Vol. XVII, Part I, 553, 555.

most of the time — sometimes on one side of the River and then to the
other Often followed the cut offs This evening we are tied up on the
Arkansas shore — and we cooked our supper on land The scenery all day
has been most monotonous Saw 12 or 14 boats to-day going up and about
all of them loaded with soldiers

Jany 22d Weather clear and cool We have been going at a good rate
of speed all day and did not stop until dark when we tied up on the Mississippi shore We saw some fine Plantations to-day and the scenery quite
good High levees on either side protect the adjacent lands from overflow
This morning we passed the mouth of White River in Ark where lie *six*
gunboats Saw the town of Napoleon at the mouth of the Ark No inhabitants could be seen The *stillness* of *death* rests on all this country Company "G" was ordered on Picket this eve and we are posted about 400 yards
out in the woods Lieut Fisk is with us. These woods are sort of *owlish.*

In sight of Vicksburgh Louisiana [sic]

Jany 23d Had a little alarm on Picket last night. Some of the 95th Ills
were on Picket also and they fired 4 shots When the cause was investigated
it was found that an innocent *Raccoon* had started the firing At the signal
for starting this morning (4 whistles) we came to the boat and were soon
gliding down the current. About 3 o'clock this afternoon we tied up at the
Louisiana shore and remained until dark

The River to-day has been confined to its channel about all the way It
was from one mile to one and a half miles wide and has been very beautiful
Where we have landed is an old field full of Cockle burs high as a mans
head and thick as they can grow The long gray moss hangs in the timber
and gives it a most sombre and mournful appearance. The limbs are covered
and it hangs in beautiful streamers often three feet long We are just above
the "great fleet" at the turning of the elbow above Vicksburgh Steamers
line the west bank far as the eyes can reach. We are a little above the head
of "Butlers Canal" which has been worked on some with the design of cutting Vicksburgh off from the River and making it an *inland* city We are
14 miles from Vicksburgh by River and 7 miles by land as the "crow
flies" [13] Below us the River has cut through the levee and a vast body of

[13] Grant's problem was to get below Vicksburg. To run past the batteries was
extremely hazardous, but was the final solution of the problem. Before that attempt
was made, however, numerous efforts were made to by-pass Vicksburg by canals.
One such canal was started by General Thomas Williams at Young's Point in 1862,

water is pouring through as large as the Des Moines River Details of men are at work *trying to stop it* We are in a most filthy and sickly condition from being on the boats so long. No hog-pen will compare

Jany 24th Weather wet and muddy The flat space between the River and the levee is knee deep in black mud. Then comes the levee which is about ten feet high and twenty feet wide at the base and this is all the dry ground we can find [14] Went out on a ramble down the River about *two* miles Saw many hospitals along the levee and there are thousands of sick men here. The levee for long distances is full of *new made graves* [15] This is a hard place for a sick man He must have plenty of *grit or die* The men on our boat sick are numbered by dozens, and few have the *small-pox* Far as I went the soldiers covered all the dry land and the boats were as thick as they could be packed They were unloading ammunition camp equipage wagons provisions as fast as it could be done in the mud

There was some heavy cannonading said to be the Rebel batteries on the Bluffs over at Vicksburgh trying to shell our men who are at work on the "Canal" [16] There are rumors of fighting below The River raised *ten* inches to-day

Jany 25th Sunday. Weather warm and a little exercise would bring the

but had failed. Another effort was now to be made to persuade the Mississippi to follow this canal, thus cutting off the peninsula before Vicksburg. "From Young's Point the Mississippi turns in a north-easterly direction to a point just above [Vicksburg], when it again turns and runs south-westerly. . . ." To cut the peninsula formed by this deep bend in the Mississippi, thus enabling vessels to avoid the batteries at Vicksburg, had, however, proved impossible, for the canal, running vertical to the Vicksburg batteries, was constantly exposed to their fire. Grant, *Personal Memoirs*, 1:446-7. Also see Adam Badeau, *Military History of Ulysses S. Grant . . .* (3 vols., New York, 1881), 1:163–6.

[14] "The winter of 1862-3 was a noted one for continuous high water in the Mississippi and for heavy rains along the lower river. To get dry land, or rather land above the water, to encamp the troops upon, took many miles of river front. We had to occupy the levees and the ground immediately behind. This was so limited that one corps, the 17th, under General McPherson [this included the 15th Iowa] was at Lake Providence, seventy miles above Vicksburg." Grant, *Personal Memoirs*, 1:444.

[15] "The camps were frequently submerged, and the diseases consequent to this exposure prevailed among the troops; dysenteries and fevers made sad havoc, and the small-pox even was introduced, but speedily controlled. The levees furnished the only dry land deep enough for graves, and for miles along the river bank this narrow strip was all that appeared above the water, furrowed in its whole length with graves. The troops were thus hemmed in by the burial-places of their comrades." Badeau, *Military History of U. S. Grant . . .*, 1:161.

[16] Grant, *Personal Memoirs*, 1:445.

perspiration out freely   Our boat moved a little up stream and we went ashore and into camp among a lot of Negro quarters which consisted of six frame houses double and a porch between.   One Co takes a house   In rear of the houses are some stables which are filled with forage   The large and fine mansion belonging to the Plantation is occupied by the line officers   We are as proud as plantation hands at our location   We brought off the boat nothing but one days rations, and our Knapsacks and haversacks   We had 4 cases of *small-pox* on board of the boat — two white men and two Negroes   They were carried off the boat and put by themselves on the levee   An attack from a fleet of Rebel Gun boats up the Yazoo river is expected at any time and we have orders to be ready to go aboard the boat at any time when called

Digging on Butlers Canal Youngs Point La

Jany 26th   Had to detail 1 Sergt, 1 Corp and ten men to work on the "Canal" to-morrow   The men do not relish the idea of having to *dig*   Drew six days Rations   The wind blows cool from the North   We are very comfortable in our Barracks   There is no *forage* here and we are dependent upon our "Uncle Sam" for our daily bread

Jany 27th   Rained about all last night and to-day is cool   We have in the Regt 12 cases of *small-pox*   The men who were on the big *drunk* at Memphis are the bluest gang that I know   They are hard to get along with and are *cussing* and finding fault with everyone   Heavy details are at work on the "Canal" to-day   Every one almost who has seen the work says it will be a failure.   *Time will tell*

Jany 28th   Last night was very cold and the ground was frozen hard this morning so that it would bear up a wagon.   I was vaccinated [17]   Had all our stuff taken off the boat   A Captain Stafford of the 1st Kansas was instantly killed at the crevasse to-day by a large Cypress log rolling upon him

[17] "Against smallpox the Army had the mighty weapon, vaccination. Since almost seventy years had passed since Jenner conferred it upon a pox-ridden world, one might suppose that vaccination had become a commonplace. . . . But many of the laity still had doubts and a large part of the population had never been vaccinated. . . . Regulations required the vaccination of recruits, and revaccination 'when necessary.' The rule was followed closely enough to prevent large-scale infection, but neglect was sufficiently frequent to account for an annual average smallpox incidence of almost 5 per thousand. Vaccination was often neglected at the training camps maintained by the states, but the principal trouble seems to have been the general failure to appreciate need for revaccination, which had not been much practiced down to that time." George Worthington Adams, *Doctors in Blue: The Medical History of the Union Army in the Civil War* (New York, 1952), 219.

Jany 29th The wind has dried up the mud and the sun has come out warm The men are on duty so much now that it is hard to get them out Working in the "Canal" is no fun Men have to work knee deep in the mud and water The officers sleep until 8 oclock and do not appear to care whether school keeps or not The men are often hurried off to work in the morning before they can get their breakfast and this makes them ugly and insubordinate There is but little discipline and the details go off swearing that they will not do anything and thus things go I do not believe our commanders know what we are here for. But they will keep the men employed until they can *think up something*

A Rumor comes that Port Hudson has been taken by our forces.[18] It is another strong hold over 200 miles below here I hear that work on the Canal is to be stoped There was heavy cannonading down the River this morning said to be the Rebel batteries firing on some of our men who attempted to cross the river Congress has passed the "Conscription Act" *Good* Nineteen cases small-pox in the Regt now

Jany 30th Weather calm warm and clear McVey and I took a stroll down the River. Men are working on the levee or "Crevasse" but with no success in stoping the water which is about 12 Rods wide and *ten* feet deep Saw Jacob Stark Sutler 34th Iowa There must be more than 100 steamboats here They line the shore for miles. Got a letter from Miss J. Keokuk. An old Negro lies in an old hut close to us and he suffers very much and must soon die Saw a lot of Contrabands just bro't in from the back country They say the Masters are running all the Negroes off to Texas to keep them out of the hands of the "Yankees"

Looking at Vicksburgh from Louisiana

Jany 31 Cloudy and warm The 1st Brigade of our Div went up the River to-day. A scouting party from our Regt went into the back country *mounted on mules* We had orders to cut wood enough to-day to last over *Sunday Strange* order that

Feby 1 Sunday: Rain rain and mud Have spent the day reading and writing Went down to the steamer "Arago" and got my dinner Capt Hanks drew a lot of Clothing and had it distributed to-day . . .

---

[18] This was just another camp rumor. Port Hudson, the last Confederate stronghold on the Mississippi, just above Baton Rouge, did not fall to Union forces until July 9, 1863, five days after the fall of Vicksburg. *Official Records*, Series I, Vol. XXIV, Part III, 499.

Feby 2d We were awakened by the noise of Cannon this morning which seemed to be but a short distance down the River. I have heard since that one of our rams ran the blockade and the Rebel Batteries did what they could to destroy the vessel [19] The Sutler who owned the goods at Memphis with which the boys were so free has followed us in hot haste and the rumor is that our Regt will be assessed $5,000 [?] as our part to be paid This may prove to be the *dearest old spree* which we have had — and one in which the innocent will suffer with the *guilty*

Feby 3d Gloriously cold for this latitude I think the sunny South is imbibing some of the frigid breath of these Northern invaders . . .

Feby 4th This morning was cold and Jack frost made us draw up our feet in bed last night like ducks in a snow drift The rain has poured down incessantly all day and at times was mixed with sleet The men on the levee have a fearful time in the mud and water I have been reading about all day in a Book called The Rivals or Times of Burr and Hamilton Our reading matter we pick up in our *travels* We captured a fine library at the Clayton House in Holly Springs It is now a "circulating" library

Feby 5th Cold and extremely disagreeable with a high wind from the NW a few flakes of snow fell We have fared badly for two or three days having nothing but hard tack We to-day got $6.70 of Company fund and we took it and bought a barrel of flour at the Commissary Out of it we got some fresh biscuit and also drew a little beef There is a cattle yard here and there are a lot of old skeletons in it which are called *beaves* [sic] It is supposed that the recent high wind blew down one of those old Texas steers and not being strong enough to get up again the Qr Master kindly *consented* to let us have the *remains* Any one who craves beef steak can be satisfied by just going down to that Corral and looking [at] those carcasses Newspapers in camp at 25 cts apiece. Work has been resumed on the "Canal" The Rebs have a 125 gun opposite the South end of the canal and cast a solid shot over now and then to keep the men awake

Feby 6th This has been a beautiful day clear and warm Drew five days Rations including 1 Brl flour Lieut Hedrick and I went down to the crevasse The men are getting the Water stoped to a small extent by putting

---

[19] This was the ram, *Queen of the West*, under command of Col. Charles Rivers Ellet. He ran the ram past Vicksburg in daylight, set the Confederate *City of Vicksburg* afire, then continued on down past Warrenton, capturing three other Confederate boats. *Official Records*, Series I, Vol. XXIV, Part I, 336–9; Part III, 39.

brush and sand-bags in the break Saw five steamers come from the North and they all landed at Grants Headquarters Rumor says we will go up the River some distance From vaccination my left arm is very sore. Vicksburgh *defiant* and *proud* sits upon the hills across the stream and dares us to come *over* We can see her Court House and all her public buildings and even the teams that are hurrying along the streets Here we are on the opposite side of a great River whose broad waters have *never* been *bridged* by human hands. Jack Frost is the only contractor who has ever taken that contract and he only operates in his own territory and makes no contracts in the Southern Confederacy If he could operate here we could soon fix those fellows *over there* We have no friends upon that hostile shore and here *we are* in this unhealthy place squatting along the levee and looking like *geese* so far as hostile intentions are concerned

Feby 7th There has been an unusual stir among the fleet to-day and some cannonading down the River At 9 oclock this evening we had orders to be ready to move on Transports with *one* days Rations Geo Reece [Rees] of Co "B" died of small-pox to-day and was burried at once

Tired looking at V. Mississippi River

Feby 8th *Sunday:* Have been waiting and expecting to go on boat all day but did not until dusk when our Regt and the 16th went aboard the "Maria Deming" She is a large boat and was built for the Cotton trade She is double deck and has an immense amount of room Besides the two Regiments we have a Battery on board and then are not crowded The sick men of the Division are on the steamer "Lady Jackson" Dan Fisher is the only one from "G" The men were very late getting teams and wagons on Our destination is unknown to us

Maria Deming Mississippi River

Feby 9th At 11 o'clock we left shore Just before we got off a flood of contrabands came in from the back country They had horses and mules and all imaginable stuff from a feather bed to a grind stone Some of the mules they sold at $2.00 per head and some they gave away Poor creatures these contrabands They fly for their freedom to the union army and we are not able to do much for them as it is all we can do to take care of ourselves The men in our camp treat them worse than *brutes* and when they come into camp cries of "Kill him" "drown him" &c are heard on every hand The prejudice against the race seems stronger than ever The Proclamation of the President has strengthened this feeling and at home the enemies of the government and the Army are *defiant* and say the Negro shall *"not be free"* There are some *fools* in our Army who think it would be a disgrace to allow a colored man to dig a trench or help us fight against his *rebellious Master* I should like to see all such *idiots* put in the *front* and in the *ditches* If any African will stand between me and a rebel *bullet* he is *welcome* to the honor and the *bullet too*

Our fleet consists of the flag ship Platte Valley, Empress, Louisiana, Arago, Maria Deming, Edward Walsh, Luzerne and a gun boat The Commissary boat City of Madison is also along We are going up stream

Camp at Lake Providence Louisiana

Feby 10th At break of day I was up and after having washed my face and taken breakfast in the cabin I went out and found that we were tied to the west shore and near a town Church spires ran up through the China trees and pointed heavenward Going up the levee I saw a lot of contrabands at work digging a great ditch or canal from the River out through the levee and they said it was to turn the water into a Lake and the Lake entered Tensas bayou which ran into Red River It is thought that a passage can be cut through for the passage of boats and we can thus *flank* Vicksburgh and land a fleet below the City [20]

This town is called Lake Providence The 1st Brigade landed here one week ago and have thoroughly occupied the place The "Provosts" came down to near where I was with "lightning rods" up and I passed around to their rear Saw a man whom I took to be a Chaplain (because I did not hear him swear) talking to a lot of Negroes. He advised them to remain with their Masters as long as possible as we could not take care of their families The Negroes did not seem to like the advice. I visited the Cemetery here and saw some very old graves dating back to the beginning of the century Some of the graves were beautifully decorated Coming back I saw a singular plant called the "Spanish Dagger" with great leaves defended by great thorns. It is used for *hedges*

[20] "On the 30th of January [1863] . . . I ordered General McPherson, stationed with his corps at Lake Providence, to cut the levee at that point. If successful in opening a channel for navigation by this route, it would carry us to the Mississippi River through the mouth of the Red River, just above Port Hudson and four hundred miles below Vicksburg by the river. Lake Providence is a part of the old bed of the Mississippi, about a mile from the present channel. It is six miles long and has its outlet through Bayou Baxter, Bayou Macon, and the Tensas, Washita and Red Rivers. . . ." Grant, *Personal Memoirs*, 1:447-8. This was another of the canal-building schemes to get around Vicksburg which would also fail.

Our boat got up steam and we went up stream about one mile and a half Here we landed and marched out from the River one and one half miles and stacked arms in a field and close to a row of Negro houses All the way to the river is one vast field white with the ungathered cotton This plantation had 100 field hands But the owner has fled and taken all the able bodied and young Negroes with him leaving all the old and infirm to take care of themselves The owner is a Genl Sparrow who is now a Confederate Congressman [21] and is said to be very wealthy His Residence stands on the North shore of the Lake and is surrounded by all that art and labor can do to make it a Paradise The Lake in front is about one mile wide and extends several miles to the westward — is deep and clear and has been the resort of Visitors from all sections

Saw one old Negro whose name is "Ephraim" and says he is over 90 years old and he does not look a day younger His head is white and he is only able to see a little His hands and fingers are hard as bone and all out of shape with unrequited toil and almost [a] century of *servitude* Another old Negro named "Peter" said he was 78 years old They were born in Va and came to this Plantation in 1825 they said We asked old "Ephraim" why his Master ran away. He said Well sah I spose he thought it better to run away den to make a bad "stan" sah

With these old people were a few small Negro children from two years old up to six or seven years There was no money in these poor old worn out slaves and the cruel and barbarous master had abandoned them to their *fate* As I looked at their worn out hands and fingers and bodies I thought of the long cruel years of bondage while under burning suns and in cold and heat they had labored for this *hellish* system of human slavery and now in the close of nearly a century they were only a few hours from absolute want and the misery of hunger This Plantation has plenty of forage and food but a few days will clean it all up We found bushels of yams and Potatoes (sweet) Genl Sparrow owned 500 Negroes

Among a band of contrabands that came in to-day was a bright little girl whose hair hung to her shoulders and was just a little *wavy* Her features were not like a Negro but were sharp and clear while her eye was *dark blue* and yet she was a *slave* Her mother was along and looked a little like she had African blood She said this was her little girl and that she had *two*

[21] Edward Sparrow was a member of the Senate of the Confederate States of America.

more daughters grown up and the *father* of all three was her *Master* who classed them all as his *slaves* A soldier who stood by and heard the Mother tell this story exclaimed in the fervent patriotism of his feelings *By G–d I'll fight till hell freezes over and then I'll cut the ice and fight on*

This morning a foraging party went from 1st Brigade and were ambuscaded by the enemy. At the first fire *six* of our men were killed and several wounded The first Kansas went out to reenforce them and succeeded in capturing 19 prisoners and cleaning them out generally.

Officers are in houses and the men in tents here Gray took a door off the Overseers house and was going to make a *bunk* of it to lie upon But Col Reid saw him and rode down to him on a gallop and asked him what he did that for Gray told him when the Col drew out his *sword* and told Gray to drop the door Gray did not drop the door but he threw it about a Rod and at the same time said take your d——d door The Valliant officer then sheathed his *bloodless* weapon and rode off Gray says he will cause *him* to have *night sweats for that*

Feby 11th Weather warm and spring like A few Peach and plum trees are coming out in *bloom* Have been mending my clothes to-day Two of the good young ladies of Indianola gave me what is called a "housewife" apiece before I left home. I kept one and gave the other away Never came anything so handy It contains needles, pins, buttons, thread and just what every soldier needs In it the needles do not rust and are always in good shape — to say nothing about the foresight and kindness of the givers. "God bless them" Attended a funeral in the 95th Ills to-day The music was the *best* I have ever heard The Chaplain spoke a few words and offered a prayer Visited a gunboat on the River She was mounted with eight Dahlgren guns — A gunboat is a nice clean place inside and the men in the Navy do not have such a *dirty* time as we

Feby 12th Last night there was a terrible rain which came in fitful dashes and showers The water stood in about all the tents this morning. Some of the men lay in three inches of water and would not have got up then had it not been for Roll Call. Company all on Picket except 1 Sergt and myself and three sick men Lieut Fisk was Officer of the Day He was strict. Men out without Passes were gobbled. A number of soldiers out on the Lake on Rafts and on the Island killing hogs were captured and the Rafts taken and the *Rafters* arrested Altogether the Naval captures consists of 4 *Rafts* and one *Horse trough* The island is a large farm and the owner came over to-day to ask protection against the invading "Yankees" who he said were killing all his *stock* and also that he had *five daughters* that he feared would be *insulted* He could have reached Genl McArthurs head quarters in fifteen minutes by rowing but the Pickets would not let him through so he went around by land in a Buggy The Negroes are bringing in wagon loads of sweet potatoes from the rich back country We traded 1 brl flour in town for 166 loaves of bread which just suits us

Feby 13th Weather warm and clear A foraging party went from our Regt to-day — out about 4 miles They brought in two wagon loads of sweet potatoes The guards are so strict now that we cannot get out to hunt our own forage Even *Gray* has about given up Only three Passes allowed per day to the Company

Feby 14th More rain last night and to-day is foggy I took Sergt Dan Embree's place and went with a squad of 28 men to work on the *ditch* But it was so wet that we could not work in the forenoon and we run around until 12 oclock Saw the Marie Deming. She had just come in from a little *trip* fourteen miles below She had on board 400 "Contrabands" taken off three or four Plantations. They were so thick on the boat that they looked like a mass of Angle worms working Big little old and young all shrieking for *liberty* They had fled with about everything that was of *no* value Old chests, trunks, and beds (a Negro never forgets his bed) coops of chickens and ducks and geese and pet pigs and all breeds of dogs Added to the darkies and all their plunder were 150 mules and horses The men are to be set to work in the ditch and the women and children to picking cotton A large force is working on the canal and we are almost through the levee when the River will flood all the back country on the Louisiana side A good many think we are only working here to cover some of the *cotton thieves* and it is not intended to make a passage here Cotton speculators follow the army like vultures follow a caravan Cotton here 20 to 30c — in New York $1.00 to $1.10 per lb

Feby 15th Sunday: Had a terrible thunder storm last night and the ground is deluged again This morning 20 men went foraging from Co "G" and they brought in 20 bales of Cotton. It was found five miles from here *under* some cotton seed Have not been outside of guard lines to-day — but have spent the day reading and writing We now have *five* months pay due Men with families at home are much discouraged and I am not far from the *truth* when I say that there are *hundreds* here that would *desert* if they had this pay Discouragements are thick and heavy upon all this army Men high in power are utterly reckless of their duty. We are having a poor Policy of carrying on the War or a poor way of executing a good Policy As it is I can but hope and pray that at least one *more year* will end the barbarous struggle

The march and desolation caused by two millions of armed men is laying waste the land Kentucky Missouri and Virginia are being trampled under the feet of the two contending armies and which must ruin them almost beyond recovery President Lincoln has called for the arming of 300,000 colored This has stirred the boiling cauldron of *treason* to the very bottom The South now threatens to raise the *black flag* and exterminate every black man found with arms. They may for a time not remember that their own *sweet* lives may go the same way. Our flag will be just as *black* as theirs if we get the 300,000

Feby 16th Ponchos and high boots are in great demand The rain poured down all last night The hog pens in Iowa do not get in a worse condition than our camp ground Guns ammunition and uniforms are in sad plight Dan built a chimney to-day for our tent but he made one great mistake — he got the wrong end on the ground and it smokes us out

One year ago such times as these would have made us all sick. But we are pretty tough and are not much affected by such small matters When we landed at Pittsburgh we knew nothing about soldiering We could not cook and we could not eat. Hard bread and *"sow belly"* we could not *stomach* Now we can digest all we can get. Never shall we forget the gloomy days and nights between the Landing and Corinth How we lay out upon the damp ground and could not help ourselves from weakness. Nine tenths of us were sick and we had to be in line of battle almost all the time We did not know how to fix our tents and how easy it was to make bunks out of little round poles such as we found everywhere and to sleep off the ground The experiences of those days learned us much We can now in two hours after we stack arms have up tents or even build houses and have up good dry bunks ready to sleep The soldier can cut 4 stakes and drive [them] into the ground take two short pieces — one at the head and one at the foot and lay down small poles wide enough to [sleep] one or two men At his head he stands his gun and cartridge box where he can reach them in the dark. On a stick having several prongs driven into the ground near his head he can hang his canteen haversack and the last thing he takes off when he goes to bed — his cap will take the highest prong　In case of a night *alarm* he can put his hand on all his fixtures　He puts his pants and vest under his head for a pillow if not expecting an alarm and if he does expect trouble he sleeps with these on and also his boots or shoes　Two flat rails with one end laid up on the *third* rail of a fence and the other end sloping out on the ground makes a good bed for a tired soldier and one which will *rest* him quicker than a feather bed　The moss of the trees is much used but moulds with a little use

A soldier in the field should never lie down in his tent until he has dug a little trench around it to carry off the water　If he wants a small writing desk he can drive a stake near his bunk and with three or four nails fasten a board on top and sit on his bunk and write to the "girl he left behind him"　The men should bunk together in pairs then the two setts of blankets will make them comfortable　Companies should be divided into Messes and one man cook for each Mess and be excused from camp duties　One man can cook for about fifteen persons. Meals in camp should be regular and three each day

Tents in this army are of three kinds Sibley or bell tents, Wall and Wedge tents　For enlisted men the Sibley is the best of all others　Is conical in shape and runs up to a peak and will accommodate ten to fifteen men with their bunks.　In cold weather a little chimney built up in the center three or four feet high will carry the smoke up and warm the tent　In warm weather the centre pole can be raised and a curb put around the bottom and the tent fastened to it which makes more room and gives all the Ventillation wanted　Wall tents are mostly used by the Officers and have an extra roof or fly attached　The tent is square　The Wedge tent is hot and uncomfortable in warm weather and is a nuisance at any time　A soldier should bathe often and change his clothes at least once a week so far as underclothing is concerned to keep Vermin from accumulating　I have seen men literally wear out their underclothes without a change and when they threw them off they would swarm with Vermin like a live *Ant hill* when disturbed　No soldier should ever complain of any detail upon which he has been called and should be *ready* at the call of the *drum* at all times looking *neat* and *clean* as possible　More men are promoted for their taste and personal neatness than from any other *meritorious* conduct — however *unjust* this may sometimes be it is nevertheless *true*　The private soldier or enlisted man is given to some strategy in the way of getting his things transported on a march

He will hide his blankets in the roll of his tent and smuggle all the stuff through he can

Whiskey and sexual vices carry more soldiers off than the *bullet* More men *die* of homesickness than all other diseases — and when a man gives up and lies down he is a *goner* Keep the mind occupied with something new and keep *going all the time* except when asleep

Feb 17th The rain never ceased all last night and has not suspended to-day Traded 1 brl flour for 160# Bread We can scarcely get our cooking done it is so wet. The mud from here to the River is about 3 feet deep

Feby 18th The rain has at last ceased We never had such a muddy camp Lieut Fisk is sick and off duty McVey and I took a stroll down the Lake and he knocked over a wild duck and caught it

Feby 19th This morning the sun came out warm and the wind blew from the southwest drying up all the surface of the *mud*, and giving us a chance to dry our clothes Everybody seems to feel better and the boys are pitching horse shoes and playing ball I had a Pass and went down town and came back through the residence grounds of Ex Planter Genl Sparrow It is an elegant place and the evergreens are full of birds singing *Merrily* Several hundred Negroes are working on the Canal and about forty picking Cotton A man named Kellogg from Memphis has charge of the cotton business and is fitting up a large Gin house here and will bale the cotton fast as it comes in.

Feby 20th Weather fine and clear Sergts Thatcher, Myers, and Jeff Hocket and I got Passes and went sailing on the Lake. We went across and called at several houses and in one deserted by the white folks we found some Negroes and a good *Piano* which had been left On the mantel piece was the *remains* of two Pictures each of *Massa* and *Missus* painted on canvas The *inevitable invaders* had been here The *culled pussons* said the soldiers had damaged them about *thusly* "Massas" *head* had been cut off and taken away and "Missus" was terribly soiled and cut. They said the soldiers had been there "*jus cussin and swarin* all de time"

Near here I found a family burying ground One very neat Monument was marked with a wreath enclosing the letters "US" and described "Here sleeps Major Felix Bosworth U. S. A. died Vera Cruz, June 9th 1847, Aged 38 yrs" Another — "William Lester son of Felix and Elizabeth Bosworth who died January 5th 1838. Aged 2 years and 4 months."

"He was the pride of his bereaved parents
The darling of his doting Grandmother
Pre-eminence was in him early shown
Heaven had marked thee for its own"

"Little Charley son of Felix and E. S. Bosworth died May 24th 1840. Aged 4 months"

"E're sin could blight or sorrow fade
Death came with friendly care
The opening bud to heaven conveyed
And bade it blossom there"

The burying grounds of the people here are generaly 10 to 15 Rods from their dwellings and are fitted up with the most scrupulous care

Going across bayou Tensas we found our way to a fine brick house on the banks of the stream After showing our Passes to the guard we went to the door and knocked A lady about 40 years of age opened the door and invited us in and going [in] we were shown into a beautiful Parlor which contained a Piano — a bed and a fine sofa The lady made us be seated and entertained us quite freely We called for some music but she said no one in the house could play as her daughter was not at home She said she had two sons in the Southern army and she said she thought they were *right* Was glad our officers had placed guards around her house to protect her from the soldiers Her name she said was Smith and said she was a sister of Tucker of Miss and wished to know if "old Scott" held any public trust (Meaning Genl Winfield Scott) Saw a good looking girl come in just as we left As we came back to camp landed a few minutes at the Island — ate dinner — went over to the cotton gin then back to the Lake and across back again to camp — to Dress Parade and to bed

Feby 21st We are almost drowned out by the constant rain which keeps falling. Drew 7 days Rations.

Feby 22d Sunday: Weather clear and warm Got a Pass and took a long walk down the Lake. . . .

Feby 23d Weather beautiful Some days ago Genl Grant issued an order against "*Card playing* and gambling" and since that time the men have taken to horse shoes and ball for amusement General Logans Division came down to-day and have landed on the south side of the Lake A heavy detail is moving the little steamer "Delia" from the River into the Lake Lieut

Fisk and I took a ride on the Lake and visited the Island Some men came near shooting us from the opposite side while firing at water fowl

Feby 24th Weather calm clear nice and warm This morning I wrote a long letter to Col G W Clark but from a matter of policy did not send it off A mail to-day brought me no letters

The Peace party at the North are making desperate efforts to bring the war to a close *any how* whether honorable or not They seem to care for no one but Jeff Davis and his side and want to know that they shall lose nothing The Conscript Bill has passed Congress There are signs of French mediation in favor of Peace But no healthy indications in favor of Peace that will be lasting More blood must be shed and thousands fall before peace can come None but the patriotic soldier can feel the impress of the tory influence at home We who have suffered the hardships and endured the fatigues and sufferings of the past two years of bloody toil can feel the *sting* of these traitors at home Peace we desire above all things but when Peace is declared let it be one that shall *endure* and the consequences of which shall never again bring us into the field

This afternoon ten or twelve houses burned down in town Some of the boys were down there at the time and while trying to save some property for a widow woman found a large "Rebel flag" The brick Church was also burned This afternoon the 11th and 13th went up the River By a Newspaper I see that Genl Sparrow upon whose Plantation we are homesteading is in the Confederate Senate at Richmond He had better be here looking after his *rails* — they are going very fast and soon the demand will be greater than the supply

Feby 25th Raining again this evening 21 men on guard to-day and some of them guarding Col Reids "fleet" of *Horse troughs* The boys sail around the Lake and pick off "peocusses" one of Sergt Grays Mexican names for graybacks

Feby 26th The rain came down in torrents last night and *five* inches of water fell Henry Metz and I took a sail on the Lake to-day and came near upsetting The Lake is rising rapidly Made out Muster Rolls to-day

Feby 27th Weather warm and cloudy Have been busy all day making out Reports Eleven Commissions came to day for men in the Regt. Four Captains viz: Capt [James S.] Porter Co "D" Capt [Christian] Landstrum Co "B" Capt [Edgar T.] Miller Co "C" Capt [Newton J.] Rodgers [Rogers] Co "E" The Lieuts are [Ensign H.] King Co "I" and Fitzpatrick same Co [George W.] Buchanan and [Emanuel M.] Gephart [Gebhart] Co "D" [John C.] Brush Co "B" [Sylvester] Rhiniason [Rynearson] Co "C" [William P. L.] Muir Co "E" There was great good feeling among the new Officers [22]

Feby 28th Weather clear warm and fine. Had muster at 3 oclock Present 50 men — 7 absent sick and 3 Parolled and same as prisoners Had to make out monthly Report to Adjt Genl Iowa and a large Bill of Clothing wanted We Muster every two months and at the end of that time there are a large number of Reports to make out and I make them

March 1st Sunday: A beautiful day Had Company Inspection at 10 oclock The *Col* went around and examined the clothing of a great many of the men and says he is going to make us all have a new suit "out and out" Our Clothes were never in so bad a condition as the present. Some of the men are barefooted and some have no pants and travel around camp with nothing on but their drawers and shirts But they are the fellows who would be in that condition *anyway* if they drew a suit each month

To day we had a large mail which brought me several letters and one from Co[l] Geo W Clark saying he had "recomended" me for 1st Lieut in his Regiment and that the Commission would be on soon. This to me is good news

The boys are having some *rare* sport these nights shelling Col Reids house Co "H" seems to lead the charge They hunt up a good supply of *brick bats* during the day and hide them in their tents and when the quiet shades of night have settled down on friend and foe and camp and field while the fog is so thick that it can be cut with a *hay knife* they venture out by plattoons [sic] and hurl a shower of bats toward the dim flickering light which comes from a window of the Col sleeping room The misiles against the frame building make the boards rattle like a great *hail storm* The Col springs out of bed and orders the guard at the door to *shoot* the first man he sees *at large* Before this time the firing party are snugly in bed and snoring away in innocence and so the poor guard himself in danger fails to find these *wicked men* [23]

[22] Names corrected as found in *Roster and Record of Iowa Soldiers* . . . (6 vols., Des Moines, 1908), 2:897–1055 *passim*. Only name not found in this official listing of Iowa soldiers was that of "Fitzgerald" of Co. "I".

[23] This is an example of the almost complete lack of discipline among the "citizen soldiers" of the army. Such actions were not peculiar to the 15th Iowa by any means. Henry Steel Commager, *The Blue and the Gray* . . . (2 vols., Indianapolis,

I think Sergt Gray and a few others in Company "G" are members of this *midnight brigade* but of course it is not my interest to *prove* it Last night the camp guards were doubled and men posted through camp to watch and *arrest* any man found out of his tent after 9 o'clock The inky darkness made it very difficult to see any one over five or six feet Along in the "wee sma" hours of the night a terrible *bombardment* commenced on the Col's house from the direction of Co "H" From some inscrutable reason Sergt Gray was up in that direction and the guards pursued him and with bayonets fixed yelled on him to *halt halt* Gray did not obey and with the guards close upon him he dodged into and out of several tents and as bad luck would follow Gray fell into one of the *kitchen slop holes* going about waist deep in the slush But he made one more heroic effort and got out — then he ran through a tent in Co "I" and emerged on the dark side leaving the guard *smelling* for him at "I" while he reached his own *bunk* in safety and was snoring away in two short *seconds* There was intervals of heavy *firing* all night but no one was found who knew any thing about it Almost any man with two pennyweights of horse sense can in this state of affairs *trace* from *cause* to *effect* Major Belknaps tent or house is never *shelled* and any man in the Regt who would do him any injury would soon be exposed and that without Belknaps help He is the only field officer we ever knew who is worth the clothes he wears

March 2d Weather clear and fine Took a ride to the oposite [sic] side of the Lake Saw two good looking and neatly dressed young ladies who are just from Kentucky having been [in] attendance at School and have now come down here to see what has become of their Plantation (said to belong

1950), 481ff, analyzes this attitude: "Americans have never taken kindly to discipline, either in peace or in war. . . . There was no military tradition in America, and little understanding of the value of rules and of discipline. This was the first major war in which Americans had ever been engaged, and it was the first to levy on the whole population. . . . There was, for example, no trained officer class, and neither government did anything effective either to use such material as was available or to train officers. . . . Most of the field and many of the general officers were appointed by state governors, usually on political grounds; a great many of these, especially in the North, earned their appointments by raising their own regiments or companies. Lower officers were customarily elected by the rank and file. . . . One result of this situation was widespread insubordination, downright disobedience, and a staggering high rate of desertion. It was not that the typical American was either disorderly or disobedient; it was rather that while willing enough to fight, he saw no reason for observing discipline when there was no fighting at hand. He had little respect for officers, as such, and many of these were not deserving of respect. . . ."

to them)   They find the Plantation *here* but nearly all the attachments gone The Plantation is deserted by their kindred and the white tents of the invaders spread over the land   Blue uniforms dot the sacred heritage and the "Stars and Stripes" float over the buildings . . .

This afternoon our long expected clothing arrived and in accordance with an order issued by the Col we are all obliged to have a uniform dress coat pants and cap   Nearly all the men drew full suits   I drew $13.49 worth We are allowed $42.00 for clothing the present year   Last year we were allowed $46.00   The Regt presented a fine appearance this evening on Dress Parade   The men were clean and tidy and the dark coats and sky blue pants looked in fine contrast   Some of the men had hats and some caps   The Col said they must all have *caps* to-morrow to appear on Inspection   An order was also read meant for the punishment of men who set fire to buildings Grist Mills &c by orders of Genl McPherson   Wrote a letter to Col Clark to-day

March 3d   Weather cool windy and clear   At 2 oclock we had Regimental Inspection and we with all our marching and fighting accoutrements stood in line until 5 oclock   The Col inspected us minutely   A few men had not caps and new Dress coats and he informed them that he would not *tolerate hats* and *old coats* on Parade   New ones had to be drawn and that *forthwith*

Here we are in the *field* and have nothing but hard *work* and *hard fighting* before us and here in the mud and water and these men with a *passable* coat are compelled to go to the expense of a new one   Some of them have wives and little ones at home who depend upon the pitible [*sic*] sum of $13.00 per month from the absent father to keep them from starvation and want while this *cornstalk* Colonel for his own glory and name can thus grab from these little ones.

Warm weather is upon us and the first trip we make all useless trappings will be cast away by the weary and thirsty soldiers   Some of the officers got a severe talking to because they allowed the men to come on Parade with hats on   Rumor says that *furloughs* are to be granted to *Meritorious* men   I *suspect* it should read *Notorious* men — as they are the ones that generaly get favors

March 4th   Cool windy and chilly   Had Company Inspection this afternoon and threw away our old cartridges and drew new *ones* and then we cleaned up our guns — our parade grounds and moved our tents and ventillated things generaly. Also drew three "Wedge" tents I *borrowed* a Pass and went down on the Sparrow Plantation on the bank of the Lake near Genl Crockers Hd quarters The little steamer "Delia" came over and had quite a gay party aboard Genl Logan, Gen Crocker, Col Chambers, and a number of ladies among the latter the *two* Kentucky girls Rumor says Vicksburgh has been evacuated

March 5th Weather cloudy. *Another* Inspection this afternoon Col Reid *tried* to drill us some and undertook to form Platoons Some Companies were larger than others and when wheeled into line again some Companies gained and some lost ground on account of not being equalized Reid did not know what was the matter nor what "ailed Hannah" until some one told him We awaited the arrival of the Inspecting officer — who was a Major He looked at our arms and many of the Knapsacks In Co "A" he found one fellow with an old *dirty shirt* in his Knapsack and he took it up between his thumb and one *finger* and made a few *pointed* remarks about it to the owner This Major could beat any man handling a gun whom I have ever seen

Co Books were examined and when done said we had passed *"bully"* Have orders this evening to sign Pay Rolls for September and October last We have had tough fare for some time. Nothing but bread and coffee, and some of the men are getting their *backs up* One fellow last night came to the door of his *tent* and shouted at the top of his voice *More Sow-belly and less style* The cry was taken up and passed all around and along the line The more the officers tried to stop the cry the more it *cried* and it is the "Password" now Perhaps years from now when looking back over these days I may remember the fearful significance of that *Midnight howl* — M-O-R-E S-O-W-B-E-L-L-Y A-N-D L-E-S-S S-T-Y-L-E Reid says this *howling* shall be *stoped* There seems to be only one way to *stop* it and that is to furnish the *Sow-belly*

March 6th Some of the Regiments are drilling to-day Was down at the River. Saw about one dozen Steamboats at the bank Saw the gun boat "Tyler" that helped save us at "Shiloh" She now has 9 guns. Immense piles of cotton lies upon the bank The Qr Master of the 17 A C has a large number of Negroes at work on all the surrounding Plantations picking cotton He pays them 1c per lb and *boards* them There has been 100 bales of cotton gathered on the Sparrow plantation. Mr. Sparrow had better be here looking after his cotton instead of preaching *treason* at Richmond The

cotton on the Sparrow place is said to be worth $50,000 ½ of this is said
to go to the govt and the other ½ to the contractor

After Dress parade Col Reid formed the Regt into divisions and then he
mounted the porch of one of the Negro quarters and read several Resolutions which he said had been adopted at a meeting of the Brigade officers at
Genl Crockers Headquarters After they had been read a vote of the Regiment was called for About one half of the men voted *Yea* about one fourth
Nay and the bal did not vote at all. When the *nays* had voted the Col
asked them to step out to the *front* and 28 men did so. Many of the *nays*
not knowing what was up did not come to the *front* When they had
formed in two ranks the bal of the Regt marched *away* to quarters. Some
of Co "E" groaned as they passed the brave 28 who were marched to the
adjutants tent where also about all the Regiment *assembled* and there was
more excitement than I have ever seen in the 15th Regt

The Col then with one of his peculiar *byena grins* asked the 28 some
questions — at the same time the Adjt took the names of the 28 Hedrick
was acting Adjutant Some of the men said they were dissatisfied with one
of the Resolutions which favored the "Proclamation of Emancipation" Some
thought themselves better than a "nigger" Finaly the 28 commenced to
catecbize the Col and soon got the *bulge* on him and he began to be *tired*
of his *elepbant* and not knowing how to *escape* out of his foolish predica-
ment Lieut Col Belknap now came to the *rescue* (as he always had to when
trouble came) and raising his voice above the din proposed *"three* cheers
for the Union" This word *fitly* spoken touched a chord of attachment and
every man joined in with a *will* with three long cheers, and wound up with
a great *Cheer for Belknap* This ended the affair which otherwise might
have ended in a most disagreeable manner Most of the *Nay* men were
from Co "H"

Marcb 7tb Weather warm and fine Last night we had a hard storm of
wind and rain Our tent came near going away. Dan and I got out and
drove stakes and held her down But we got well drenched A forage train
went out to-day but found nothing but fodder The Rebs have captured
the "Queen of the West" the best gun boat we had Troops are going
through Yazoo Pass on opposite side of the River and we shall probably
go soon [24]

[24] The canals at Vicksburg and Lake Providence both having proved failures,
Grant here turns to another effort to reach Vicksburg. The Yazoo River, which en-

March 8th Sunday We had a terrible storm of wind, thunder, lightning and hail about 5 oclock this evening The wind blew a hurricane and drove the rain right through our tents At 10 oclock we had Reg Inspection Reid inspected guns Knapsacks &c He is one of the [illegible] . . .[25] Lieut Evans Co "A" was officer of the guard yesterday and last night Col Reid went to the Guard house and found the Lieut *asleep* and all the men The Col brought away *two guns* with him and to-day sent the Lieut under arrest and took his sword from him News to-day that our men have taken Yazoo City and 9 Rebel transports Have been reading to-day a book called "External Evidences of the Bible"

March 9th Weather cool and cloudy On dress Parade this evening in 13th I saw a man marched up and down in front of the Regiment with a guard on either side of him and on his back he carried a board with the word *"Thief"* The board was painted black and the letters white The music played was the "Rogues March" The victim was tall and slender and did not seem to be more than 19 years old His offence was stealing $48.00 from a comrade. He will be marched in front of the Regiment several evenings in succession. All the men seemed to feel sorry for the unfortunate fellow By the decisions of a "Court Martial" here several men have been sentenced to hard labor in Penitentiary at Alton Ills for the term of their enlistment Two men were jerked out of the ranks in our Regt this evening because they came on Parade with their pants in their *boots* and one of them had a *scotch* cap on Grave offense that "Hugh T" One man in the 11th Iowa for *cussing* the name of the President of the United States and calling him a G-d s-n of a B—h and a black abolitionist and said [if] he had the power he would *shoot* him — has now to carry a 20 lb ball

ters the Mississippi just above Vicksburg, follows a northerly course parallel to the Mississippi, changing its name from Yazoo to Tallahatchie to Coldwater, at its various forks, until it reaches the vicinity of Helena, Ark. There it is connected with the Mississippi by a "narrow and tortuous bayou," known as Yazoo Pass. The Union forces hoped to get boats through this pass, and thus down the Coldwater-Tallahatchie-Yazoo to the rear of Vicksburg. McPherson's 17th Army Corps had been ordered to this area, but lack of transportation kept him from joining the expedition, which began on February 24, and ended in failure on April 8, 1863. Badeau, *Military History of U. S. Grant* . . ., 1:168ff; *Official Records*, Series I, Vol. XXIV, Part I, 371–421.

[25] Here words evidently failed Boyd, and he indulges in a series of garbling wording resembling — on paper — modern double-talk. There seems to be some system to the lettering, so possibly it may have been some sort of private code which he and Dan Embree understood. From Boyd's previous comments on Col. Reid, no doubt what he has to say here was scurrilous in the extreme.

2 hours per day   One Sergt in 10th Ohio Battery for getting drunk on guard was reduced to the Ranks and made to wear a ball and chain 30 days

March 10th   More rain fell last night   Drew five days Rations   Sugar was saturated with oil so that we could not use it.   Somebody *shelled* Col Reids quarters last night and *made* it quite lively for the old gentleman   It was no doubt some of the *Nays*   The Free Masons held a meeting last night. Most of the Officers belong   Tim Ridlen received his discharge Papers last night   He has not been fit for duty since he was shot in the left arm at Corinth last October . . .

March 12th   Weather beautiful and clear   This morning Col Reid came to my tent and with one of his *grins* beckoned me out   He then showed me a *"Commission"* which he said had come for me for an office in the 34th Regiment   He said he had already *forwarded* my name for a Commission in my own company and supposed I would not want to *leave*   The Commission dates to March 1st as 1st Lieut Co "B" 34th Iowa Vol Infty   The Col wanted me to come to his quarters this evening and let him know what I intended to do.   So at dark I went over and told him I should go the first opportunity and that he *once* could have given me a Commission but seen fit not to do so   He smiled a kind of *Aligator smile* and I bid him an *Aligator adieu*   I believe about every officer in the Regiment has congratulated me on my success in *flanking Hugh J*   They say I have served him right for the way he has used me   Will start for Benton Barracks Mo in few days to join 34th Regt   About all of Co "H" are in the Guard house to-night and those not in are *shelling* the Col Headquarters and the Guard house

March 13th   Weather fine clear and warm   Rec'd Sept and Oct pay to-day   The men were glad to get even that much but would rather have more.   A part of Co "H" men were escorted by Lightning rods to the Paymasters   None of them refused their pay on that account I believe

Farewell to Co "G" Lake Providence La

March 14th   I have [been] very busy all day getting ready for departure I went to Major Clarke of Genl McPhersons staff to obtain an order for transportation   Sergt Sheffield and [I] got into a skiff [and] with two good sailors we started with sail up across the Lake   The wind blew very hard and we had a tempestuous voyage of three miles down the Lake   With the aid of Col Belknap (who is acting Provost Marshal for this Corps) we obtained an order on the Chief Quarter Master of the 17th A. C. for transportation to Memphis

This afternoon I spent settling up my business and at sundown bid farewell to Co "G" Depressed as I may have felt at bidding good bye to friends at Home when leaving for the War there never was a *sadder* moment in my short life or in all my experience than when I said *"good-bye"* to those *faithful boys* with whom for 19 long months of suffering of trials and common misfortunes — amid hunger privations and scenes of peril and death we had stood together as one man. How often they had divided with me their meager fare and little comforts I had been Orderly Sergt from the 1st day of organization down to the present time Seldom an hour or day when I did not know where every one of them was — whether sick or well, absent or present. At all the Roll Calls by day or by night their faces were before me like a picture on the wall I know most of their little troubles and trials in the Army and at home and often gave them a word of advise or sympathy and too often stood between them and *higher* authority in matters concerning their welfare As I took them by the hand and felt that electric thrill of sympathy which comes from a *true* heart I could not but realize that I should rather be a non-commissioned officer with such *friends* than be at the head of any Regiment *without them*

Surgeon Gibbon ordered an ambulance to take me with my trunk to the Landing Sergt Dan Embree came down and helped [me] on board the "City of Madison" If Justice is done Dan Embree he will get the Commission which Reid said should be mine if I consented to remain [26] Next to myself I should rather see Dan get a Commission than any other man who lives True faithful and honest he never shirked a duty . . .

About 9 oclock several steamers came from below. Sheffield who has likewise just received a Commission in 9th Cavalry is a Sergt in Co "D" where by Reids persistent meanness he tried to keep him But like my own case he *failed* We went aboard the steamer "Spread Eagle" and took a comfortable state Room Not however until two or three military officers had examined our Papers and pronounced them O K As I go upon deck and cast one farewell look at the shore I can see hundreds of Camp fires burning brightly through all the surrounding country and I instinctively ask myself if the *Roll has been called*

Good-night

Cyrus F. Boyd

[26] Dan Embree was commissioned second lieutenant, March 7, 1863, and first lieutenant Aug. 27, 1864. *Roster Jowa Soldiers,* 2:936.